Draw a Mullet on a Monkey

and 100 Other Silly Drawing Ideas

A Photo Doodle Book For Artists of All Ages

ISBN-10: 0692334718
ISBN-13: 978-0692334713

Get ready to doodle, imagine, and be creative

as you follow these prompts to create some

incredibly wacky works of art.

Give the giraffe a bunch of bowties.

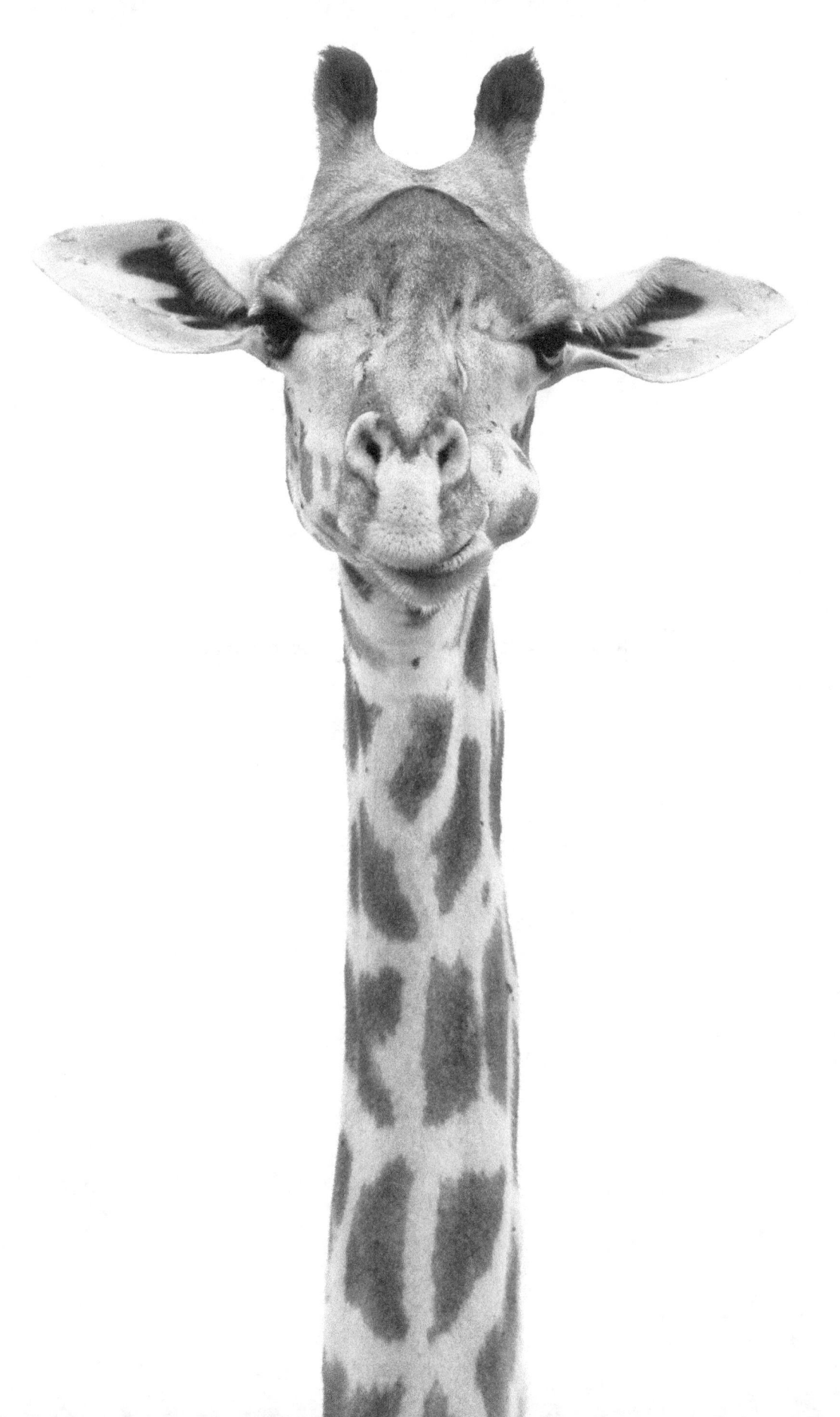

Draw a spaceship in a bottle.

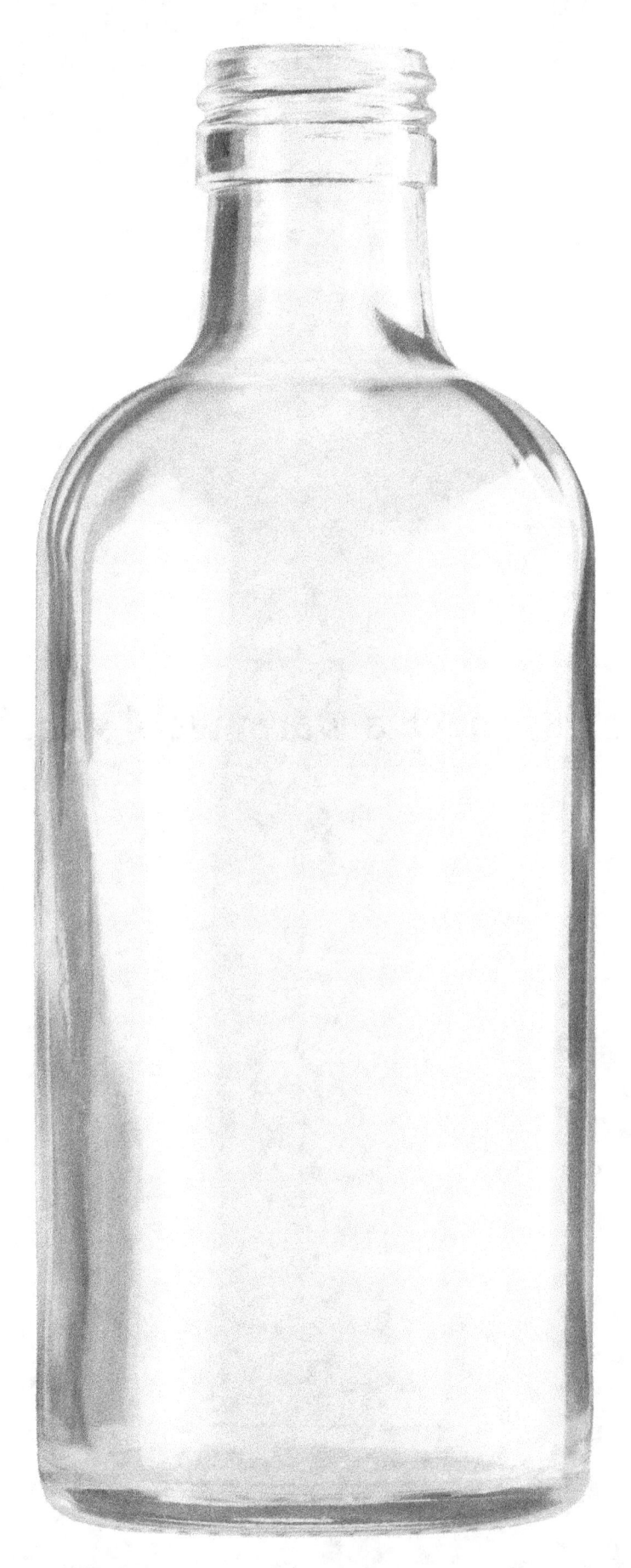

Give this sheep a warm wool sweater.

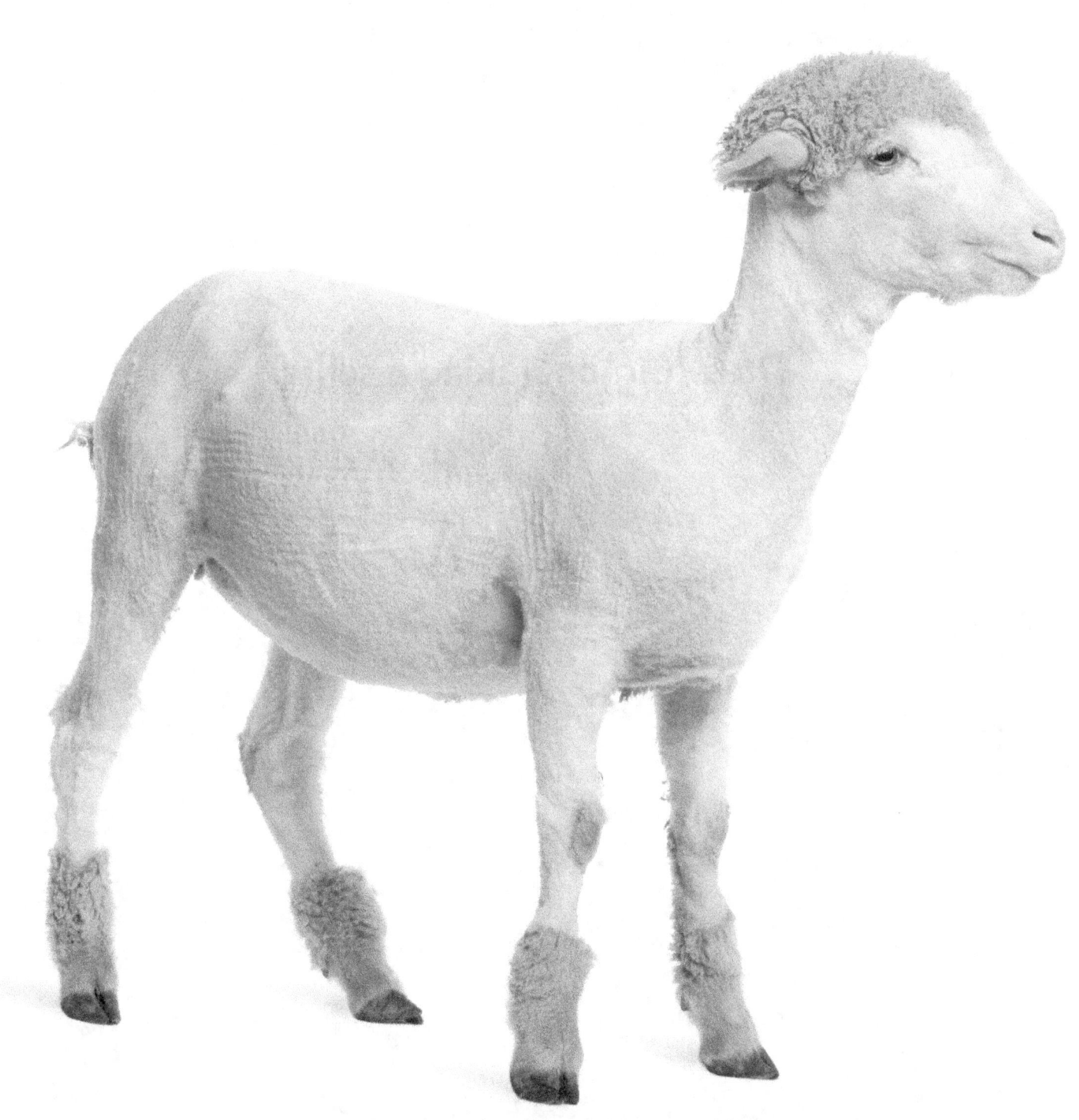

Draw Bigfoot taking a selfie.

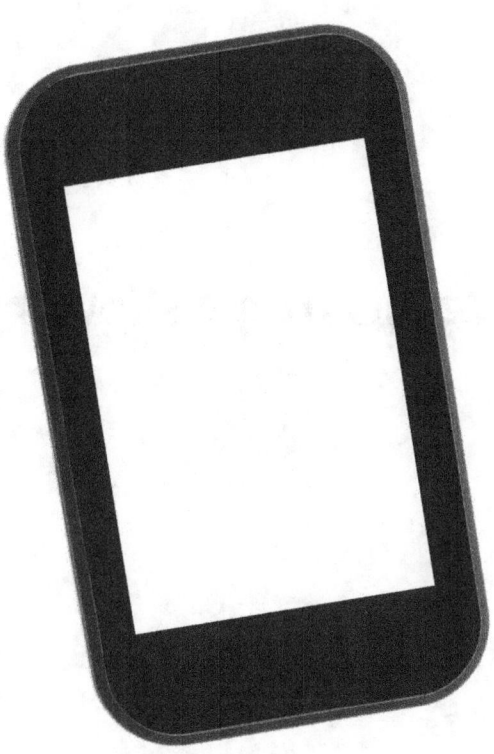

Give this frog a shower cap and a suds—filled bubble bath.

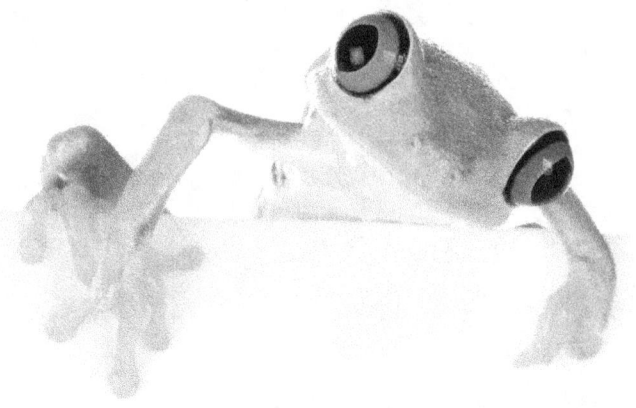

Give this leopard a big, bushy beard.

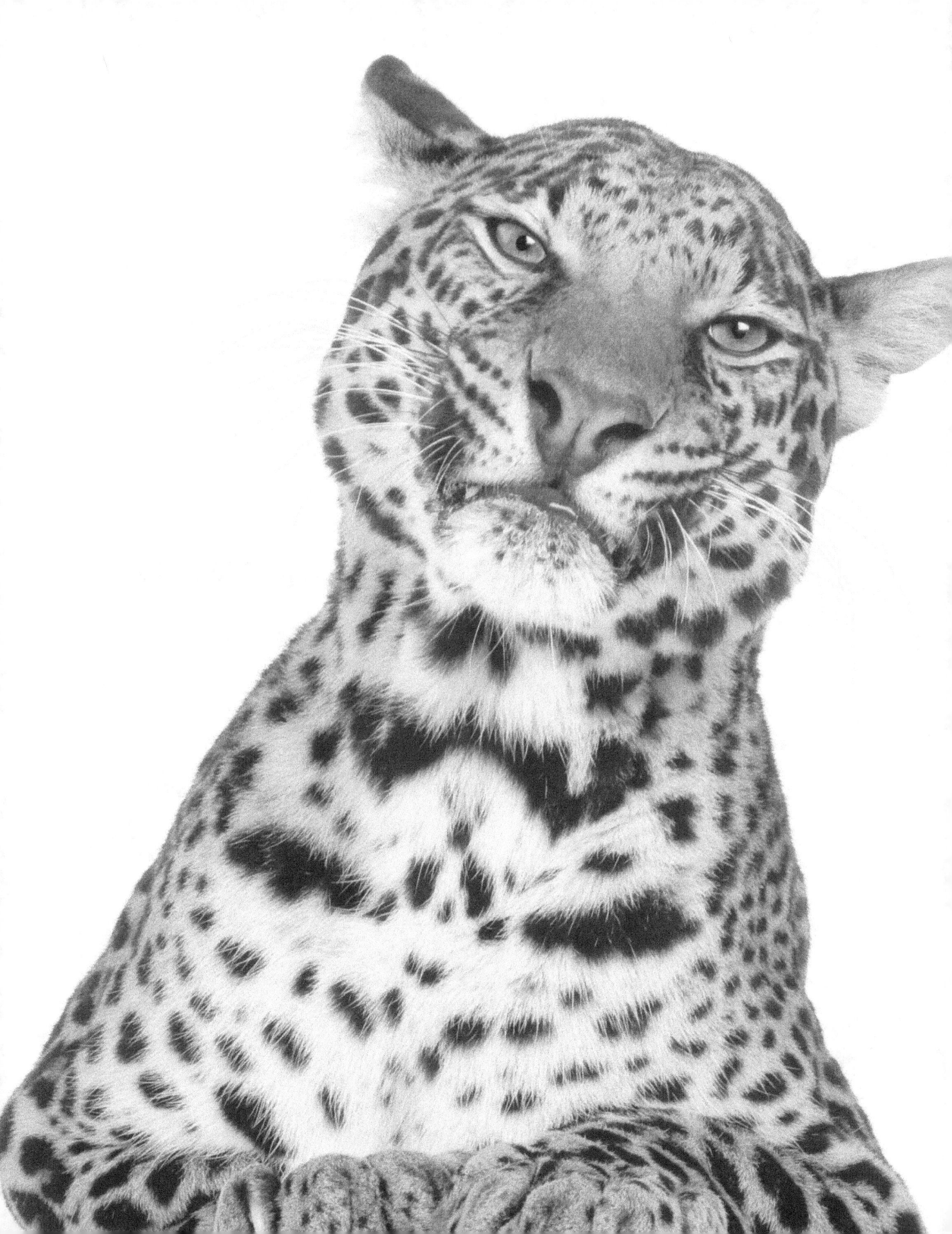

Make this parrot the captain of a pirate ship.

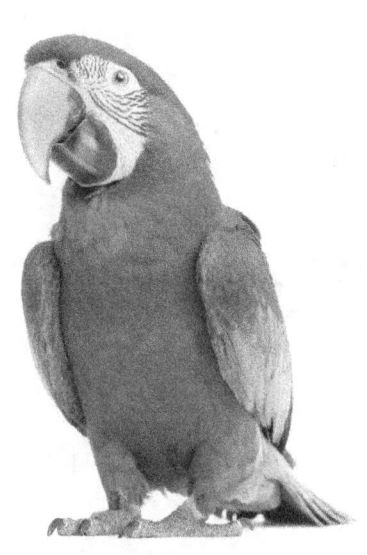

Draw this horse soaring through the sky in a hang glider.

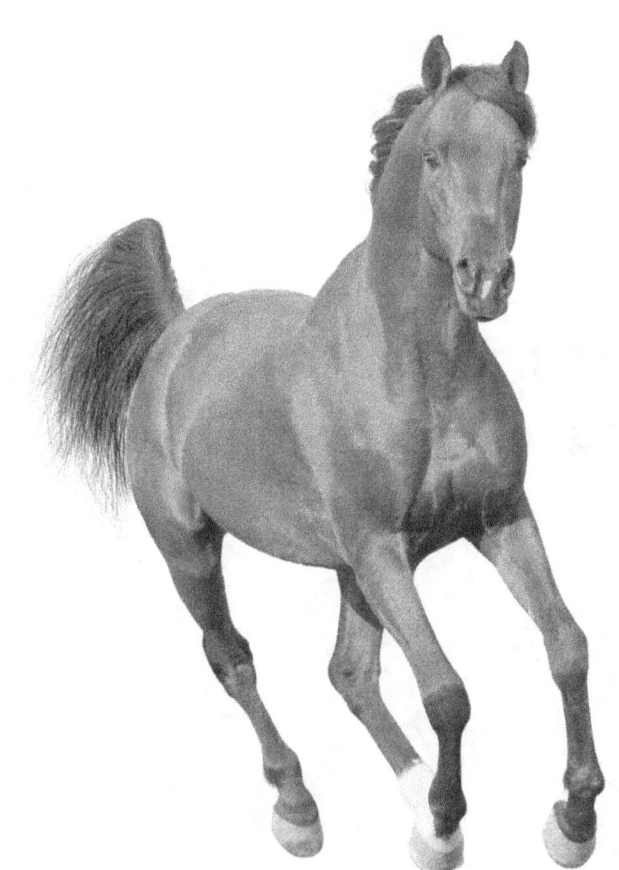

Put this bear in a canoe and then draw him
paddling down a river.

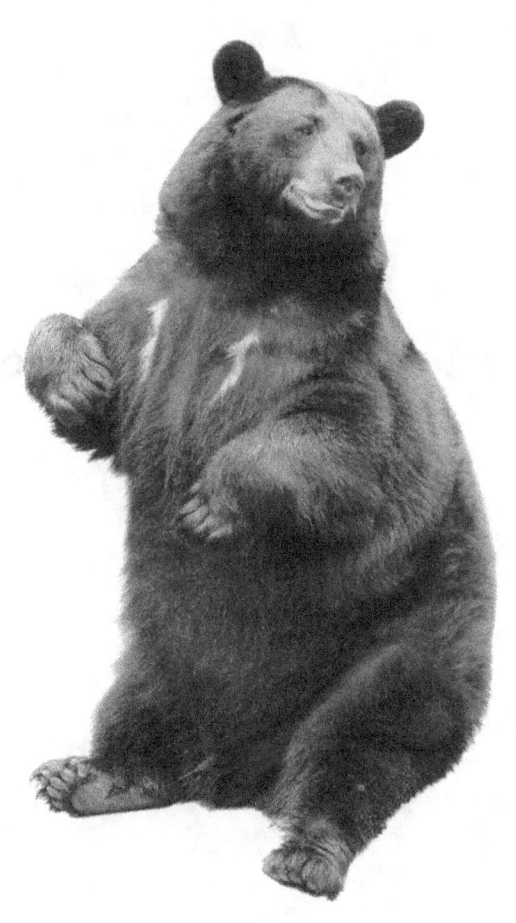

Draw a cowboy riding this balloon animal.

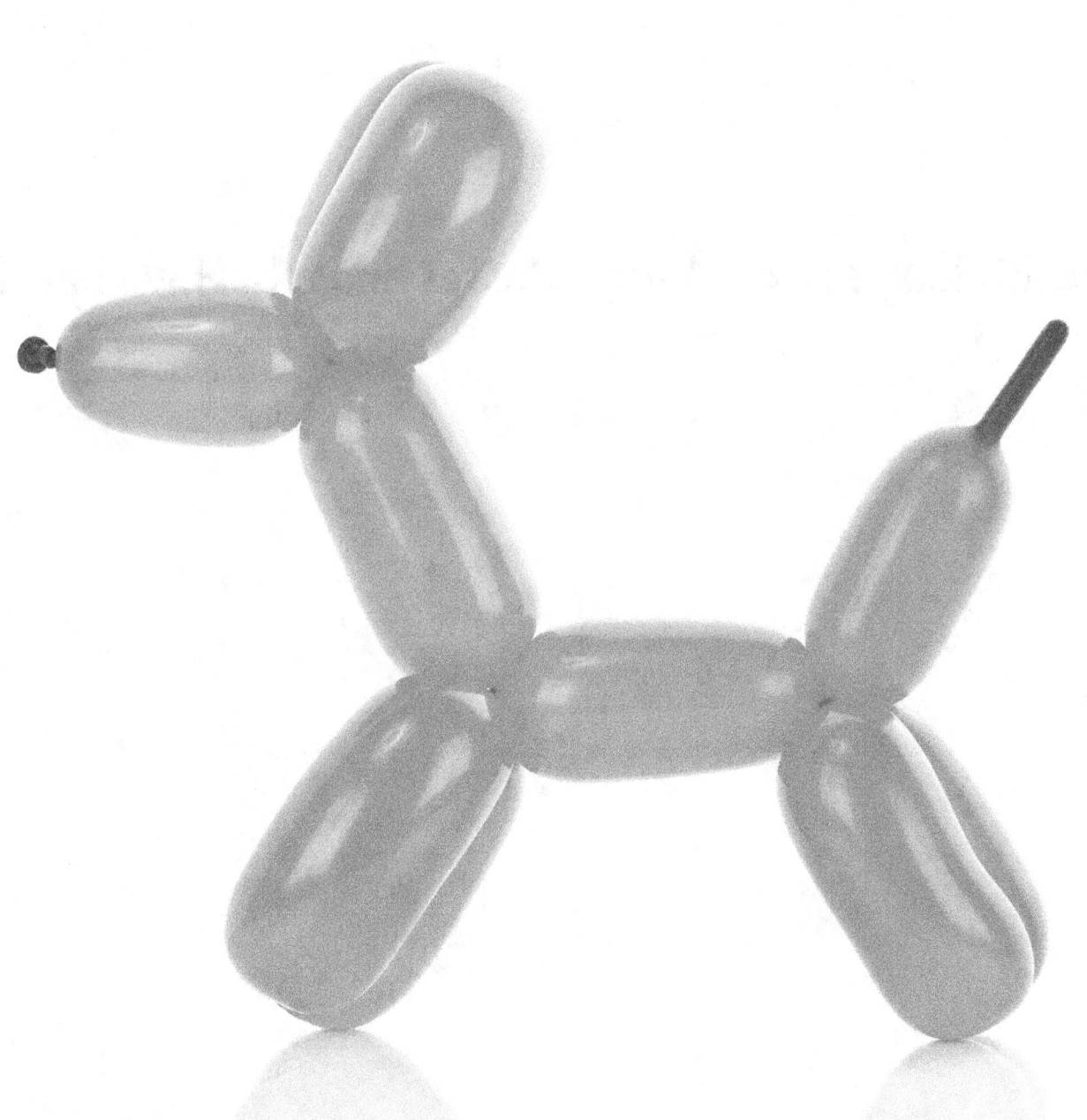

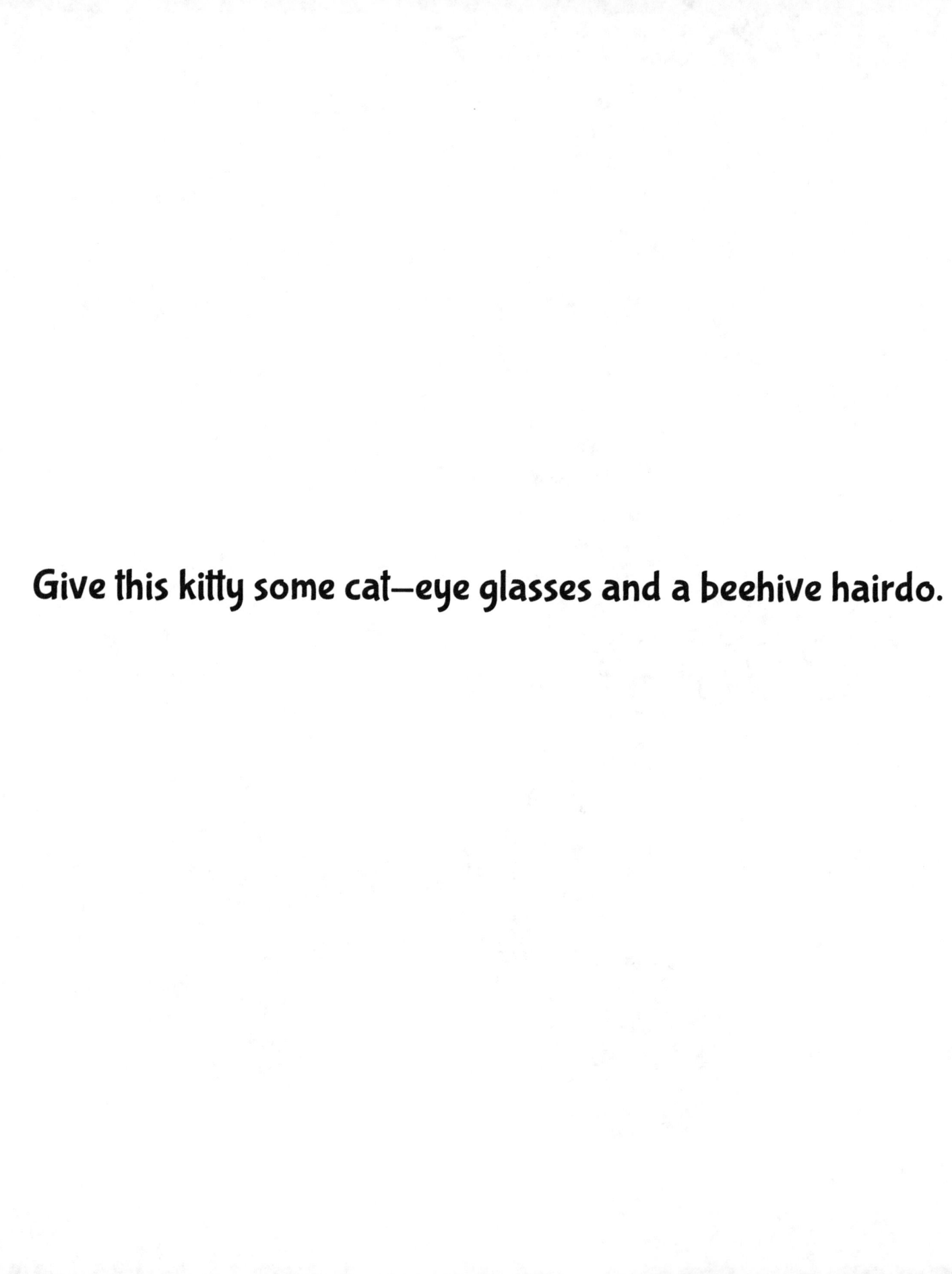

Give this kitty some cat-eye glasses and a beehive hairdo.

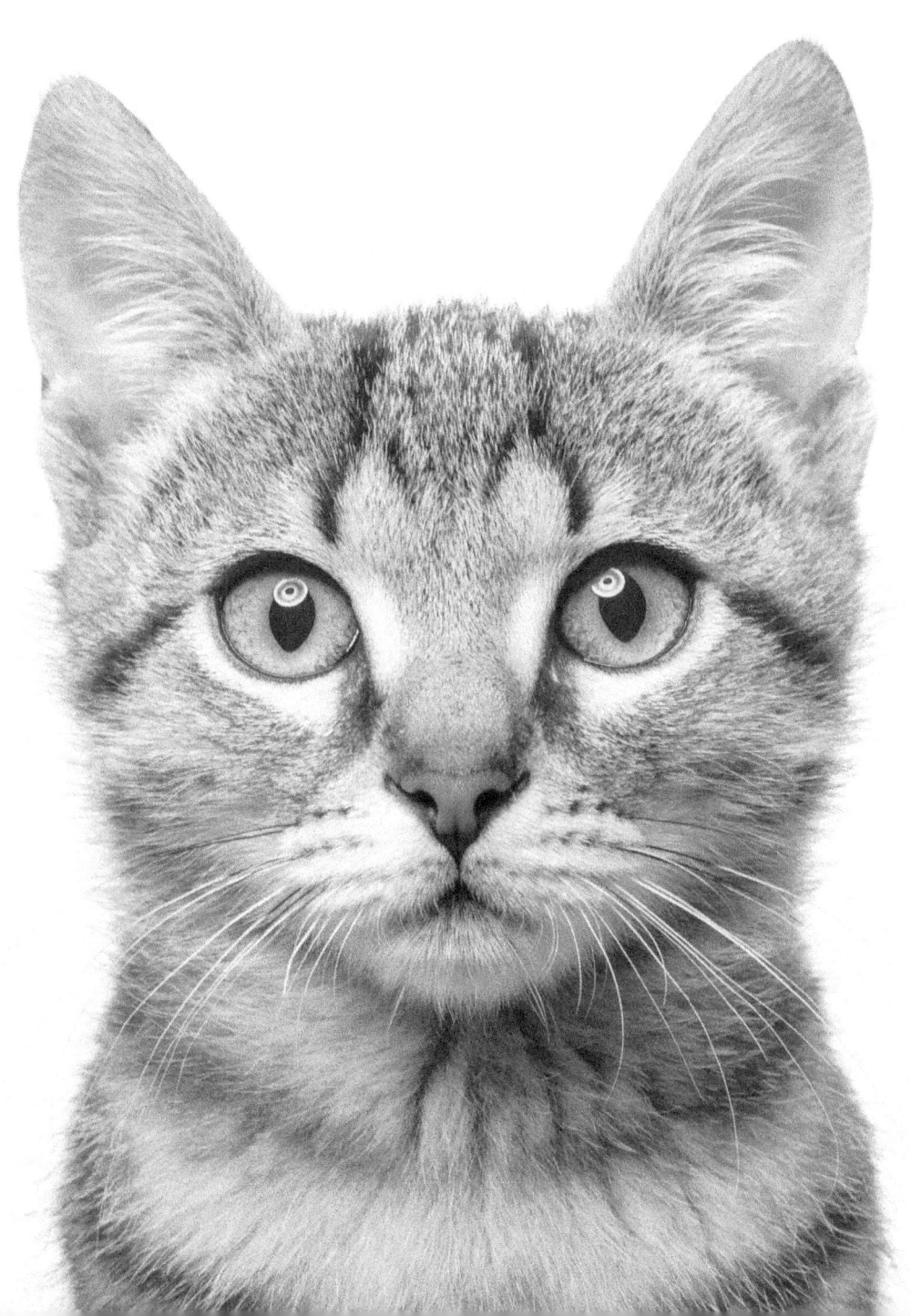

Transform this prairie dog in to the sheriff of a Wild West town.

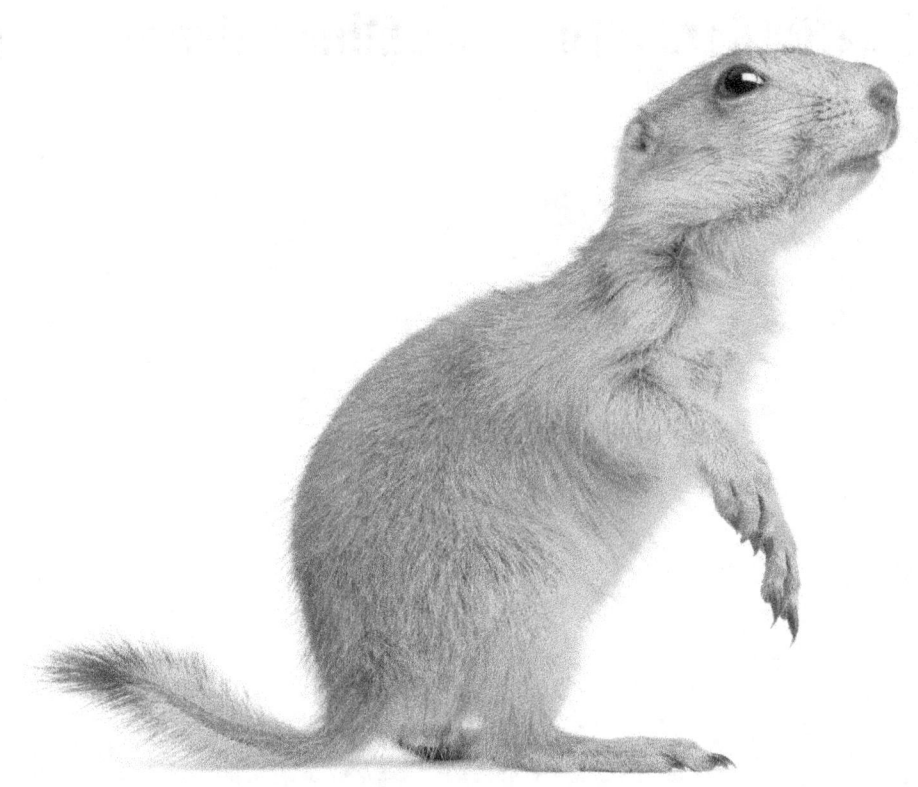

Give these firefighters a fire—breathing dragon to battle.

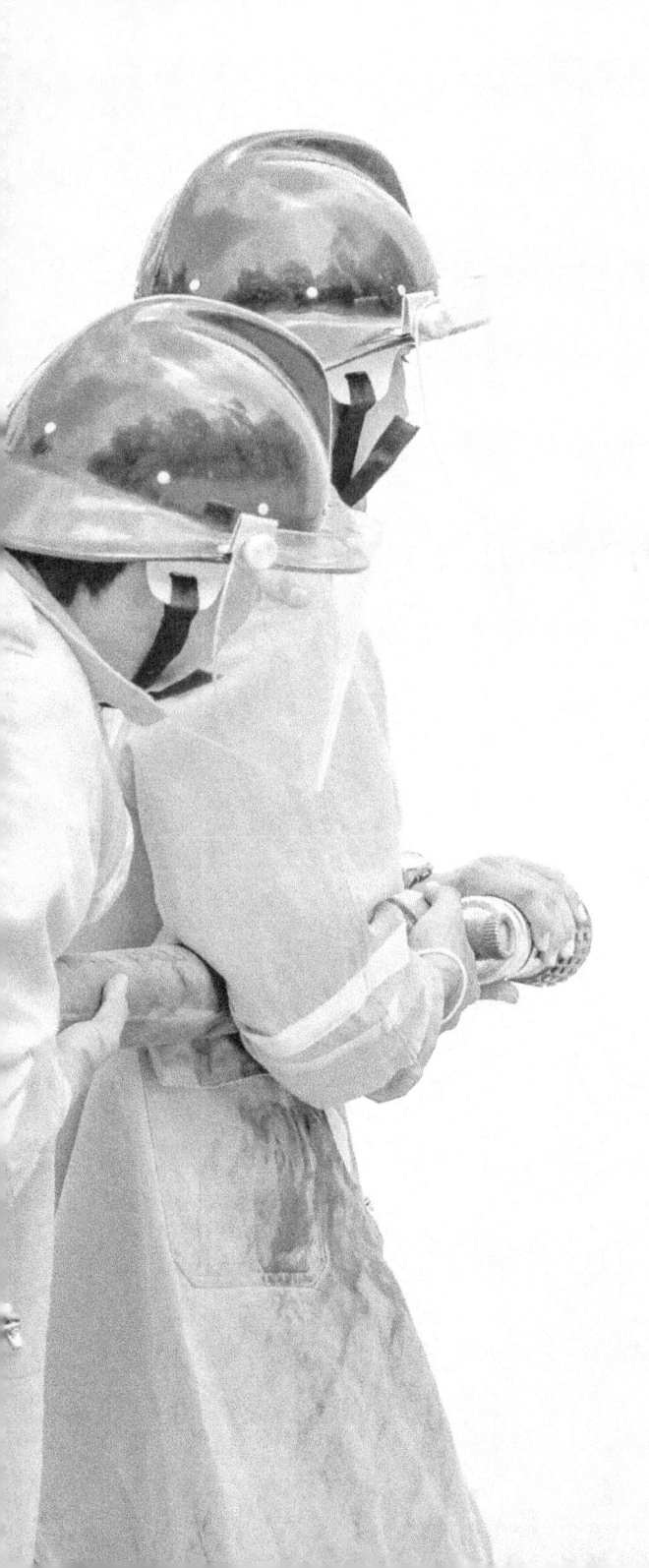

Turn this lobster in to the drummer of a sea—life band.

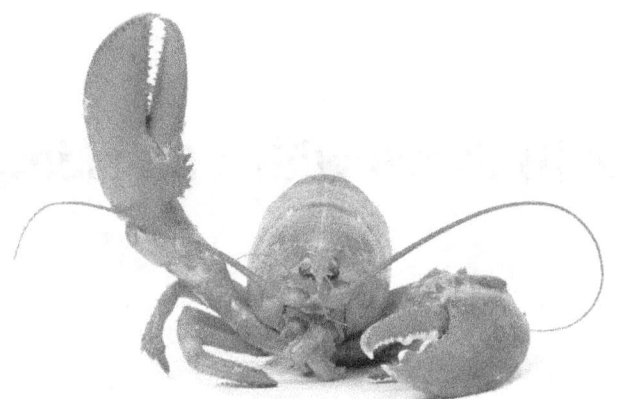

Fill the fishbowl with a tiny kingdom.

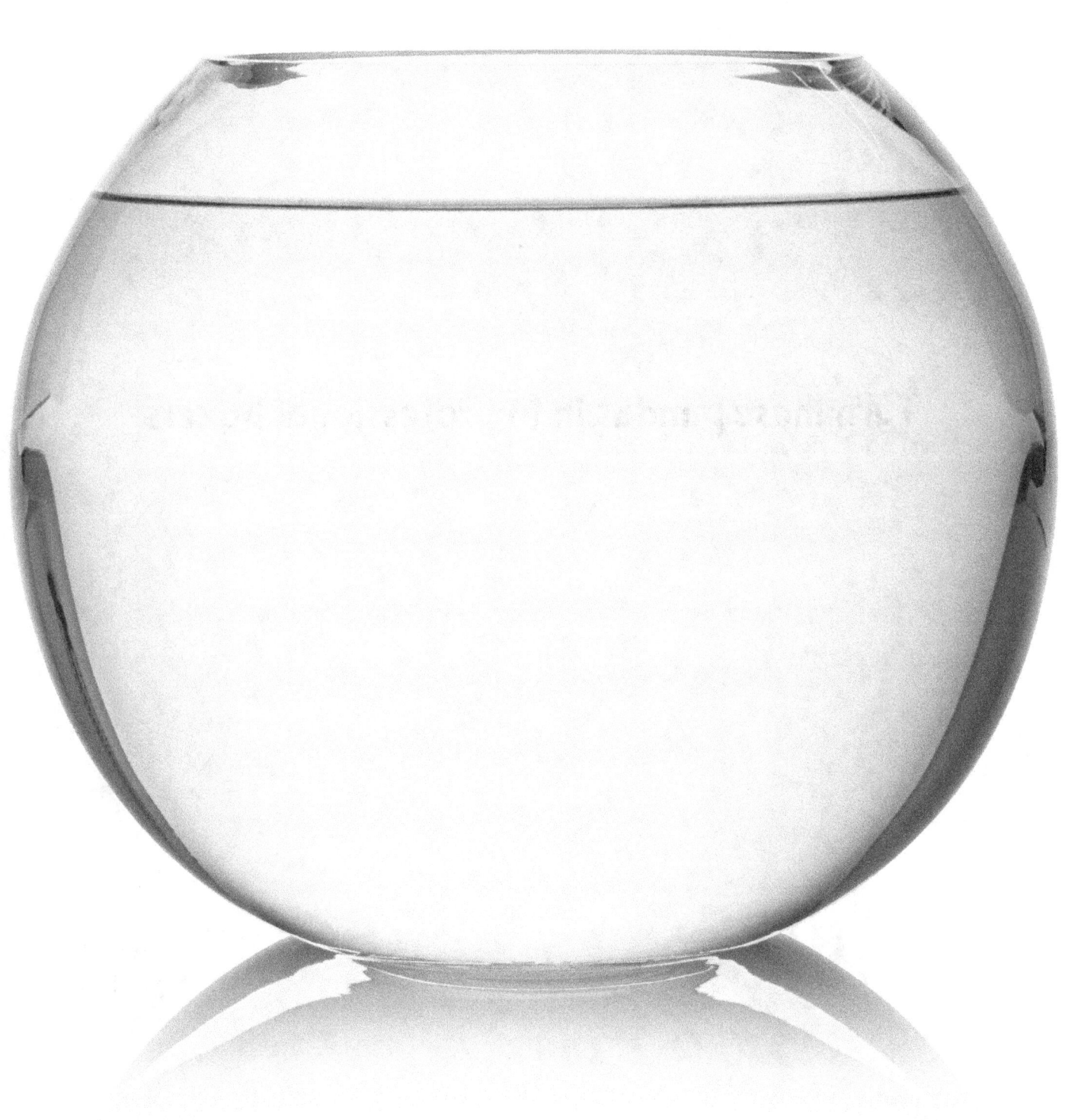

Turn these pandas in to professional boxers.

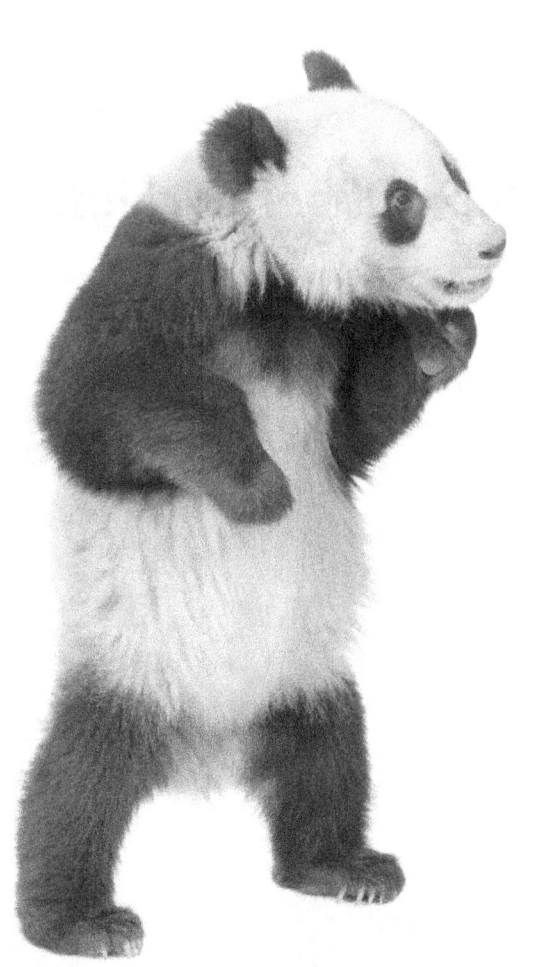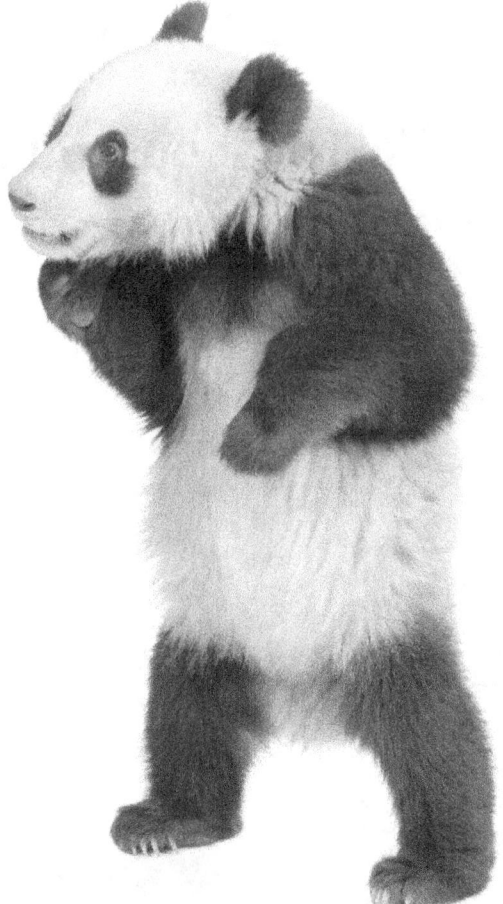

Fill the lagoon with a bunch of rubber duckies.

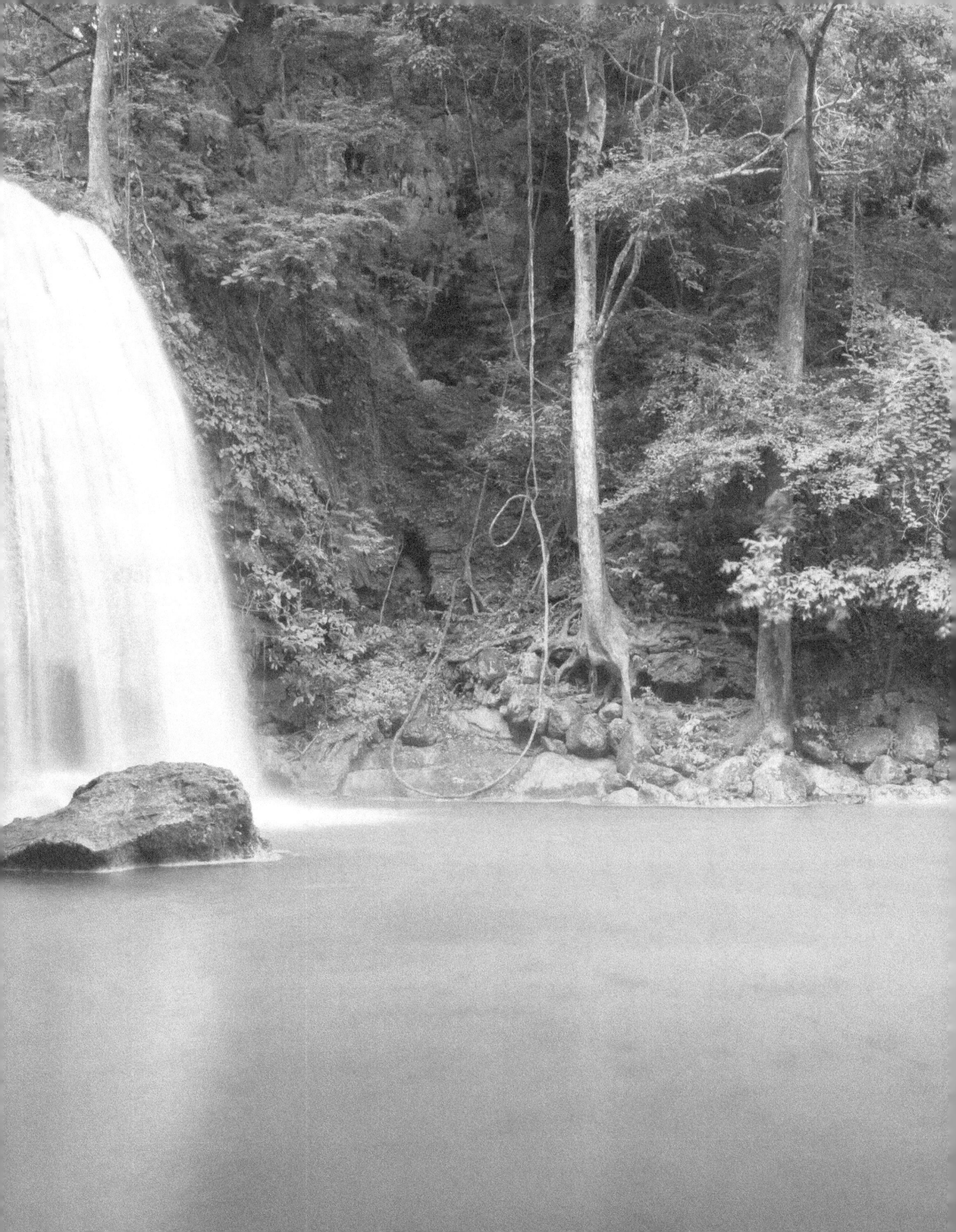

Turn these little frogs in to a bunch of ballerinas.

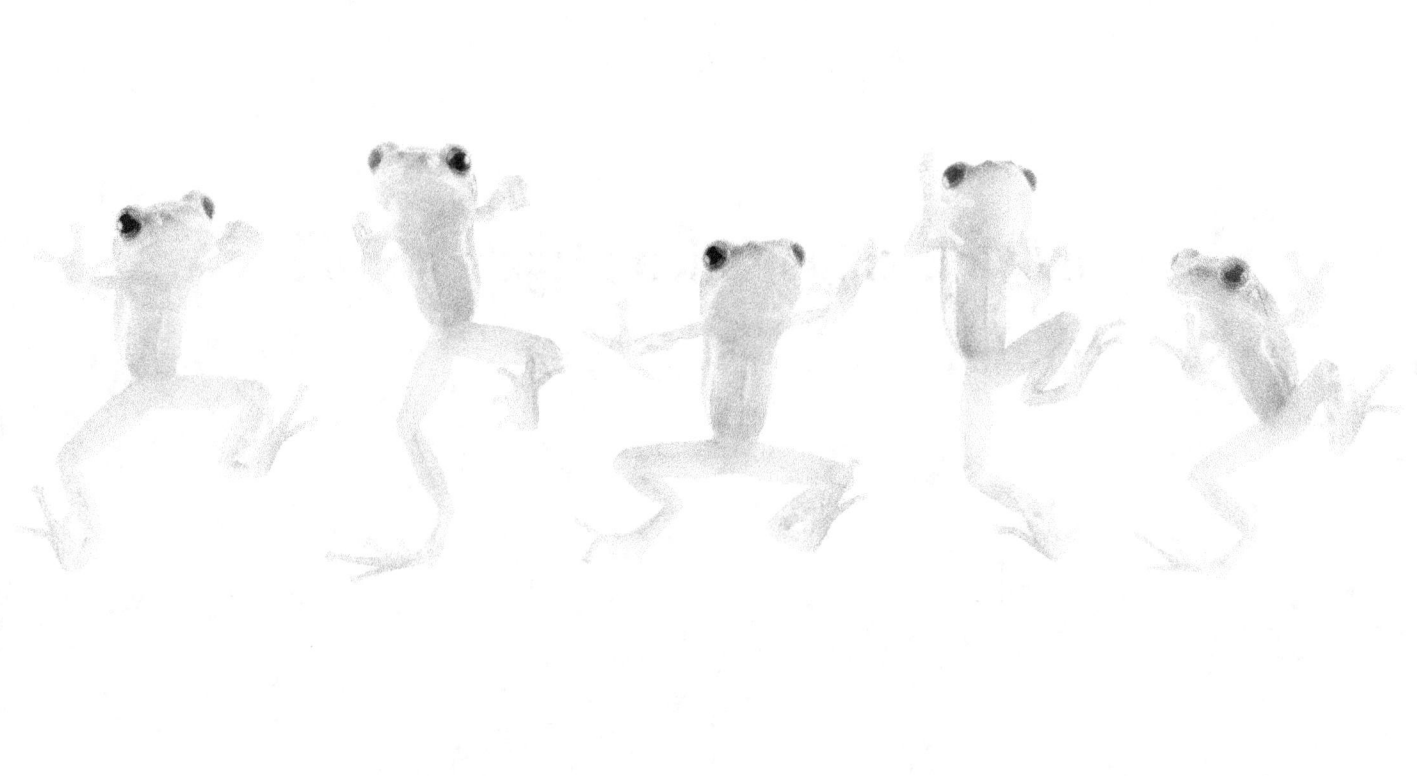

Give this chipmunk a bicycle to ride.

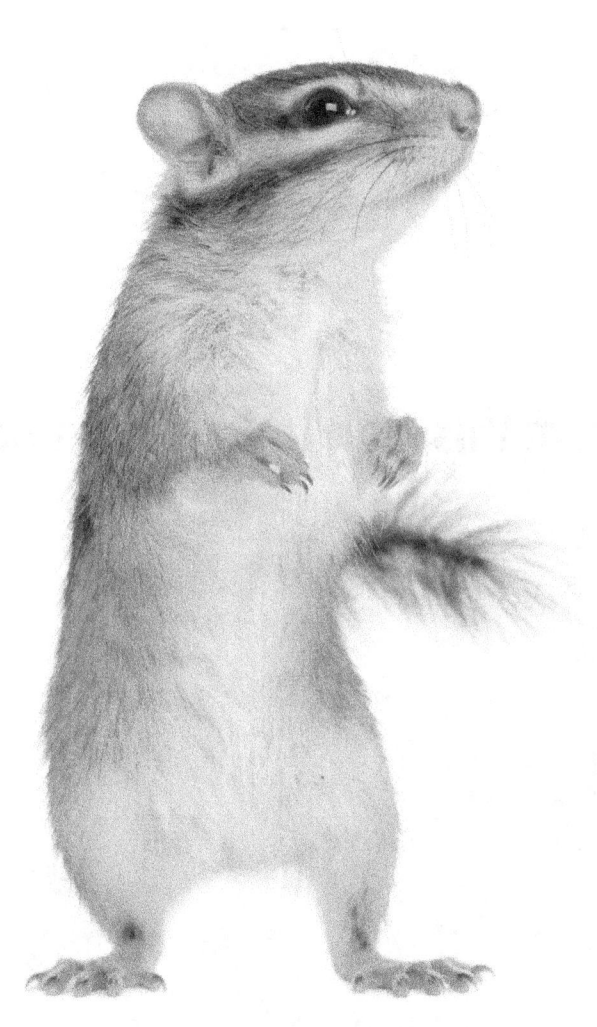

Transform this dog in to a hula dancer.

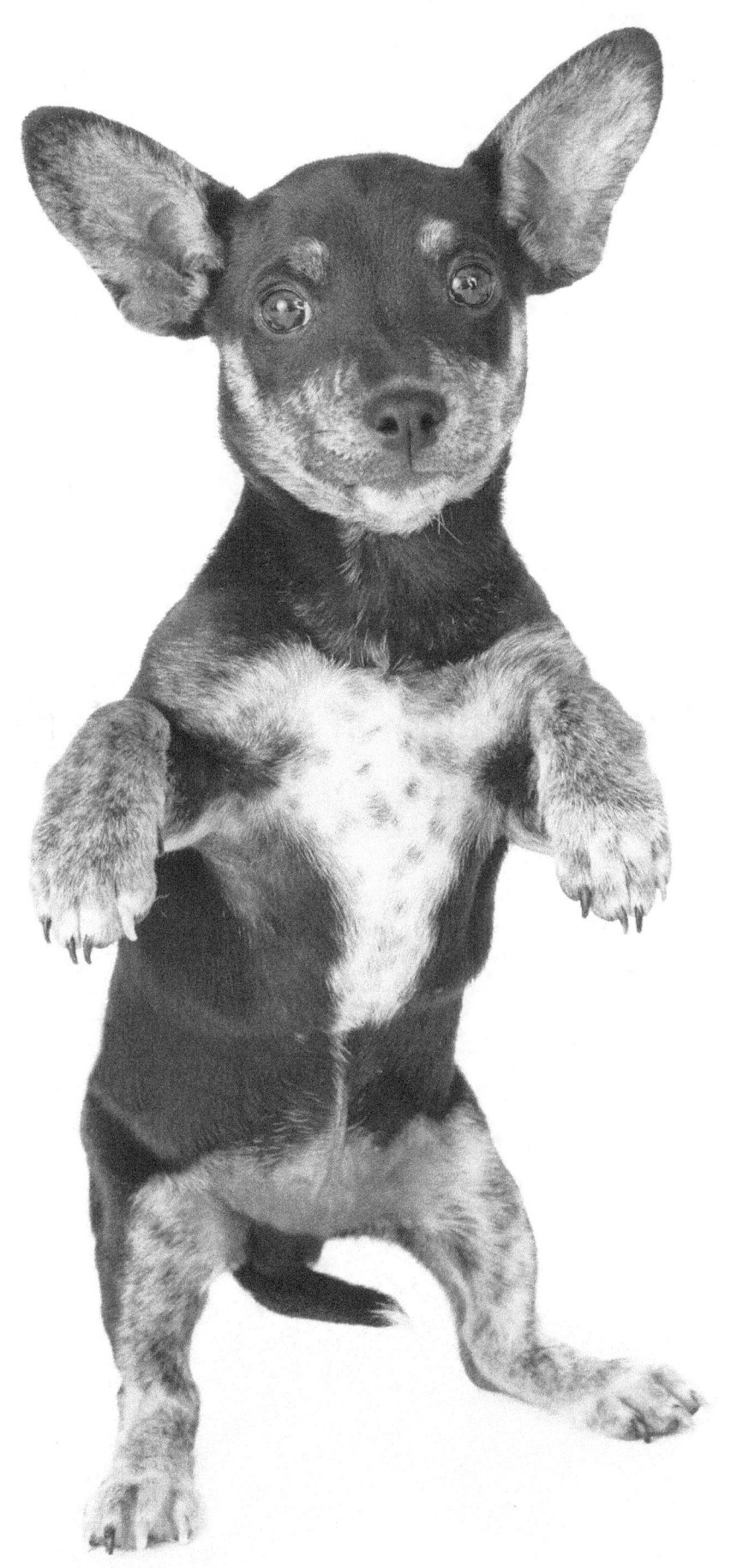

Draw this cat floating on an inflatable raft in the middle of a pool.

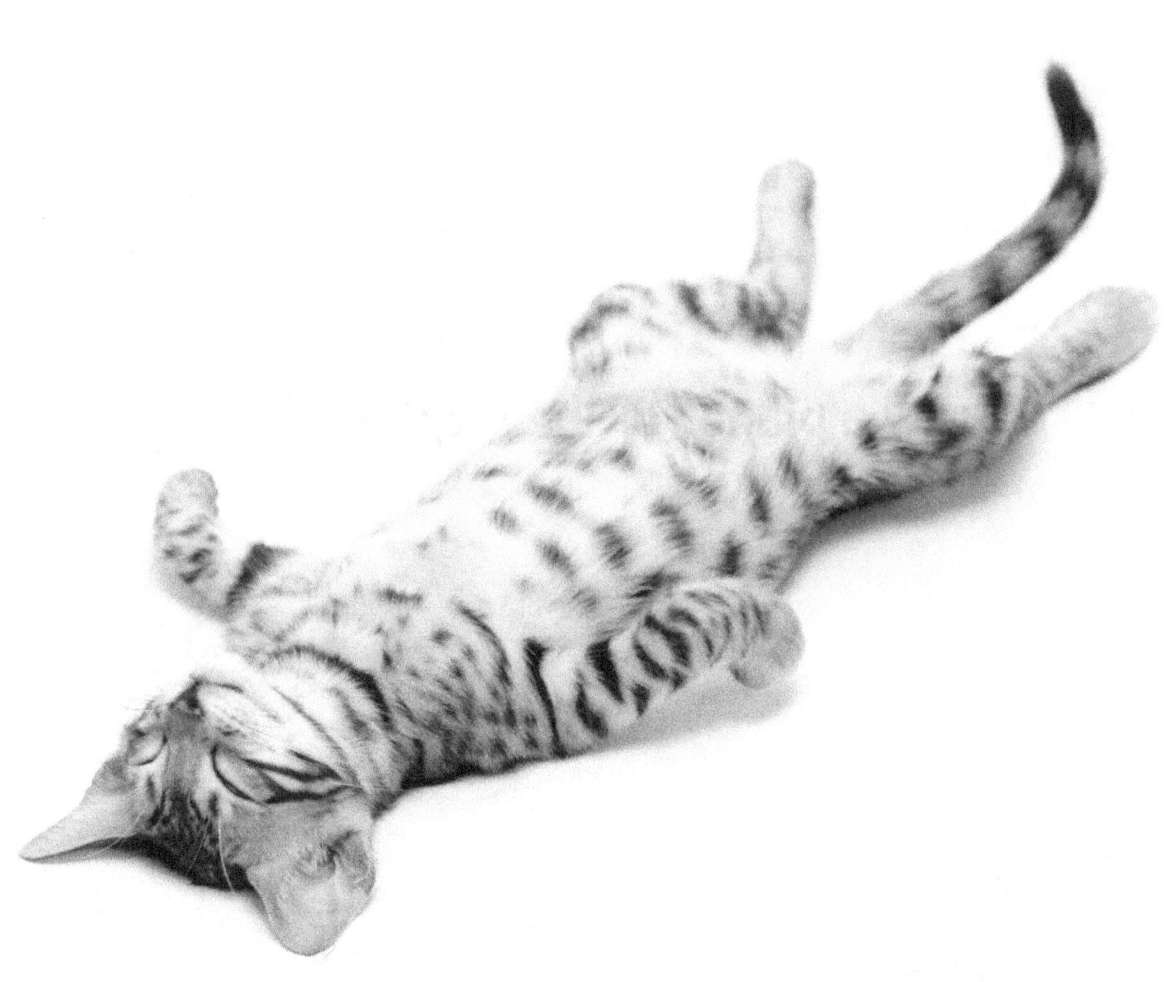

Draw a piano for the elephant to play.

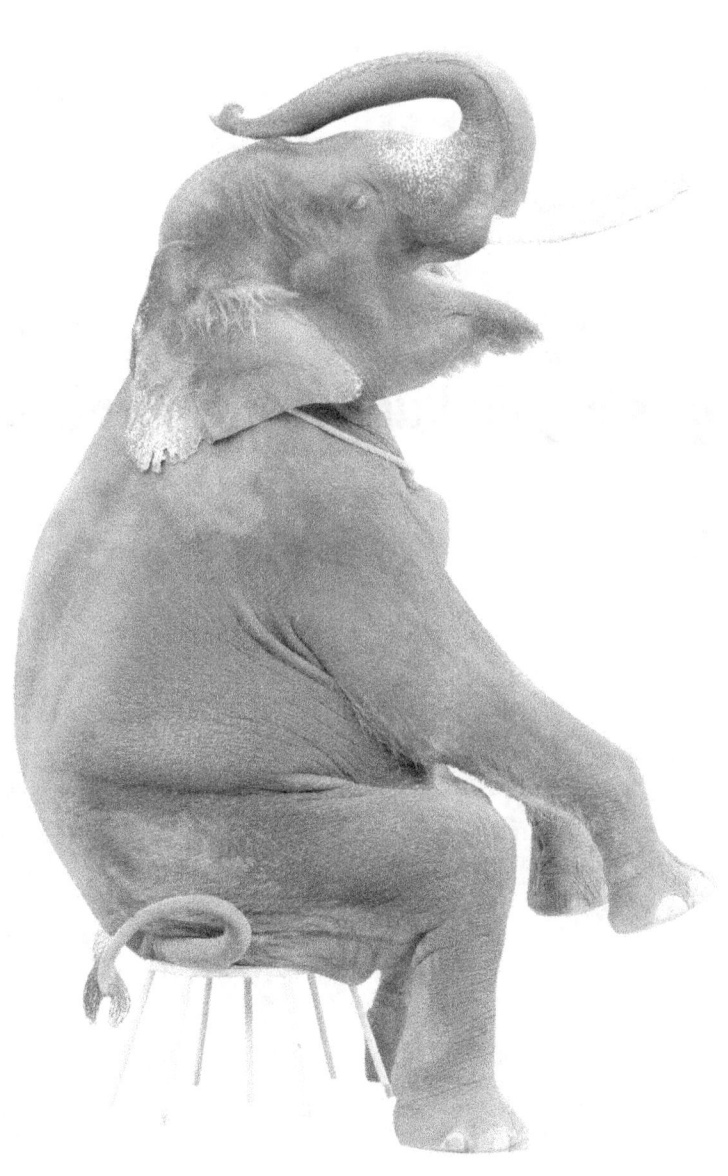

Draw a bunch of pigs snuggled under the blanket.

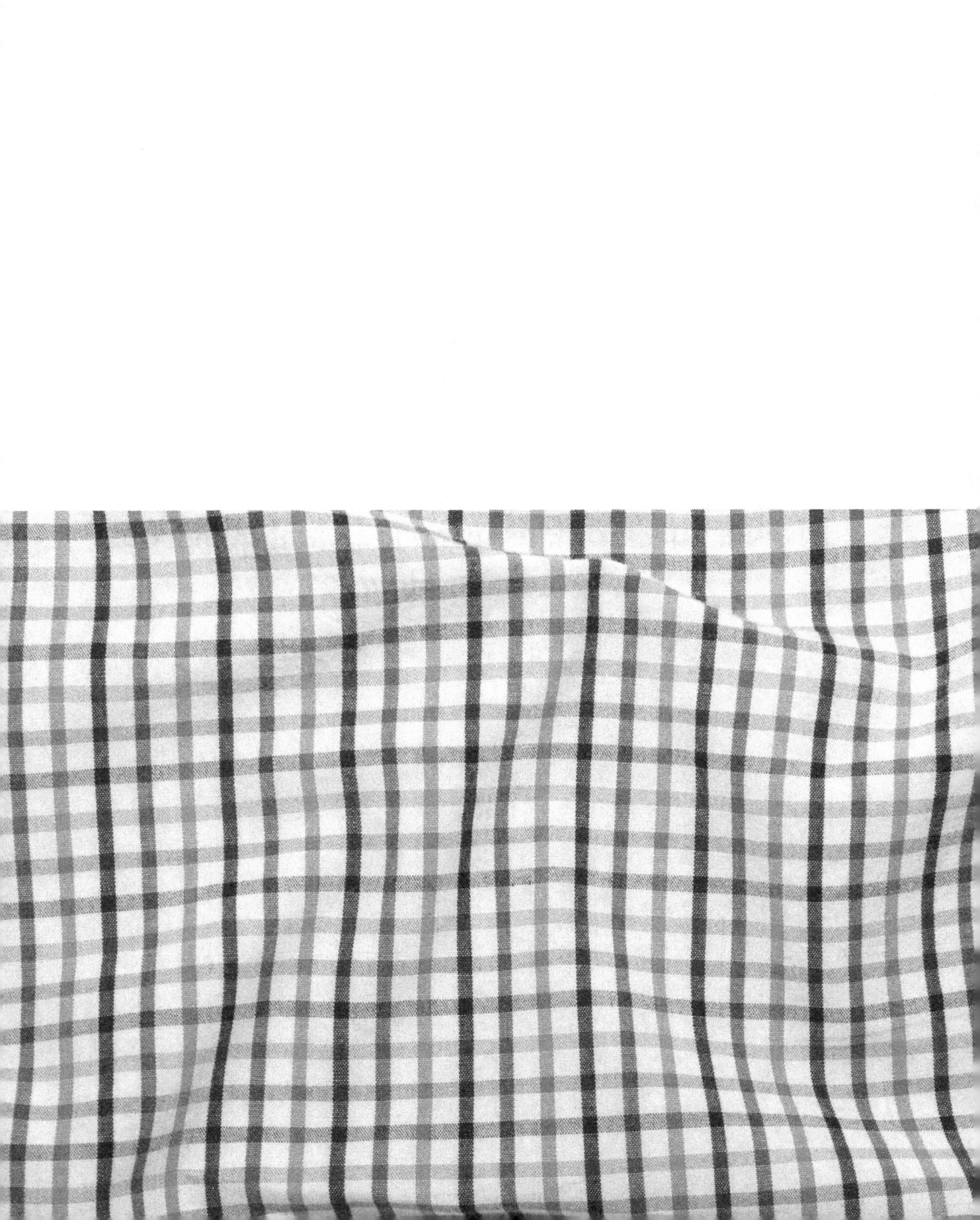

Draw a bunch of kids using the giant gumdrop
as a trampoline.

Give this ant a barbell to lift.

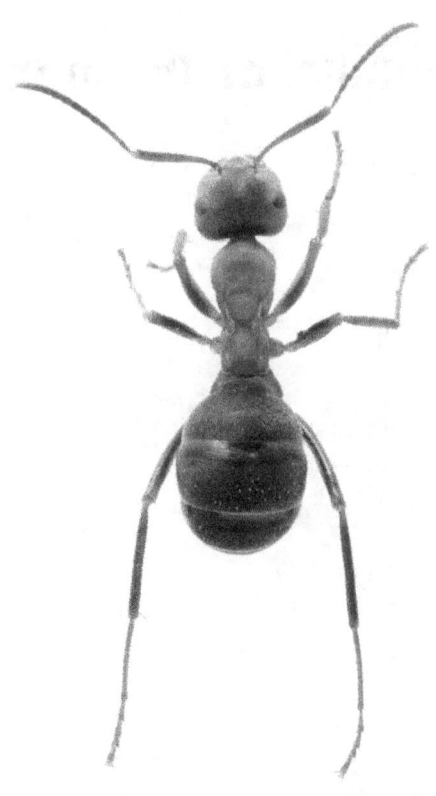

Draw a mullet on the monkey.

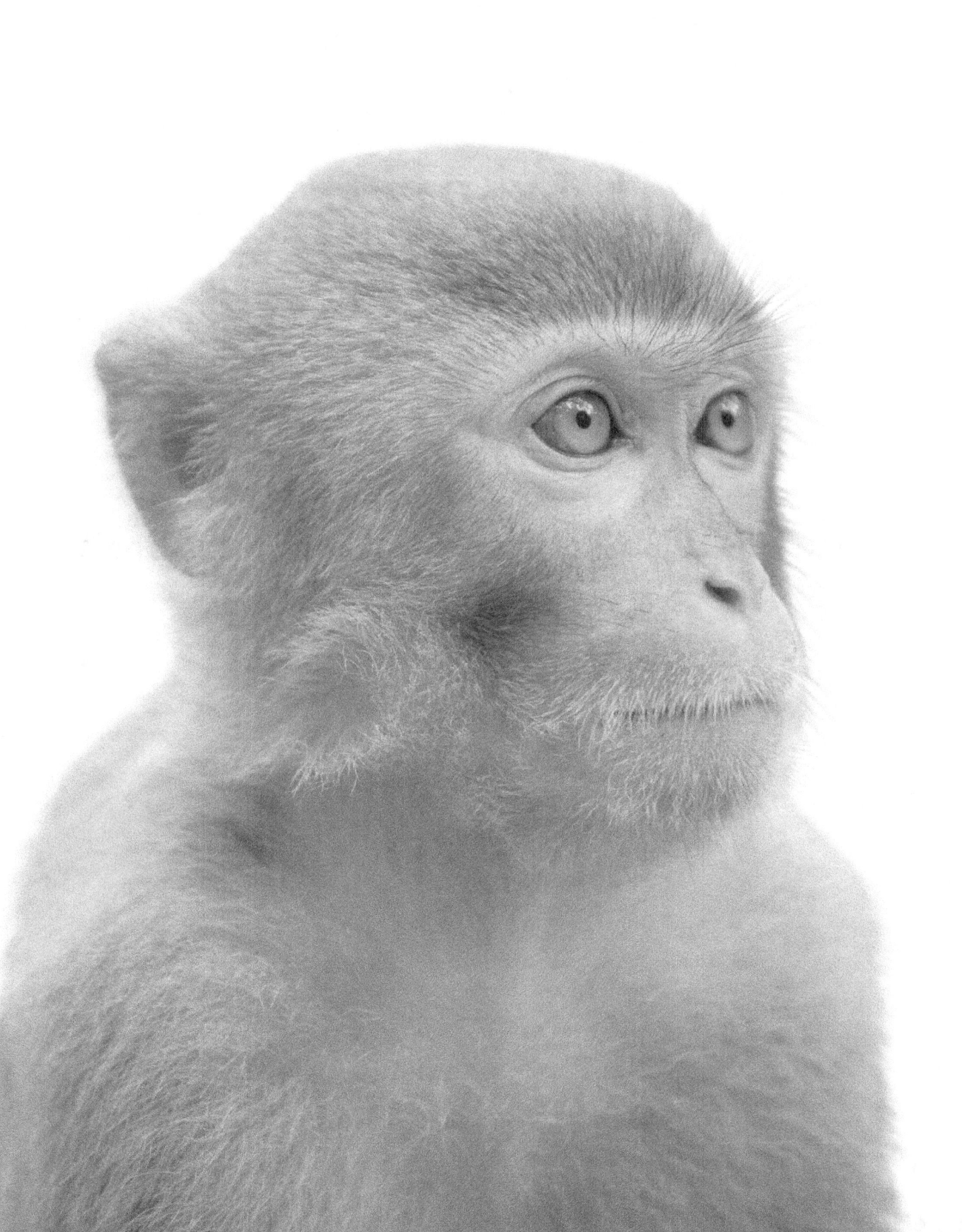

Dress the cat so that it looks just like Puss in Boots.

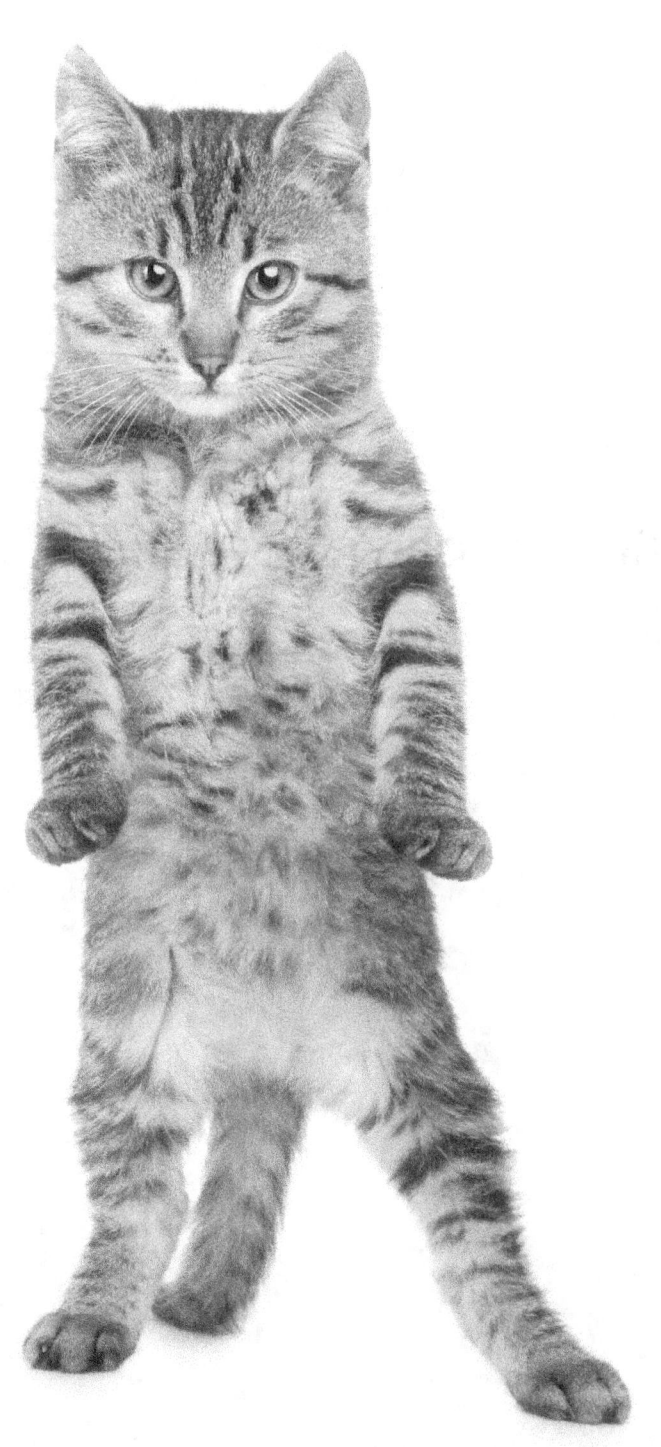

Give this squirrel a hobby horse and a ten–gallon hat.

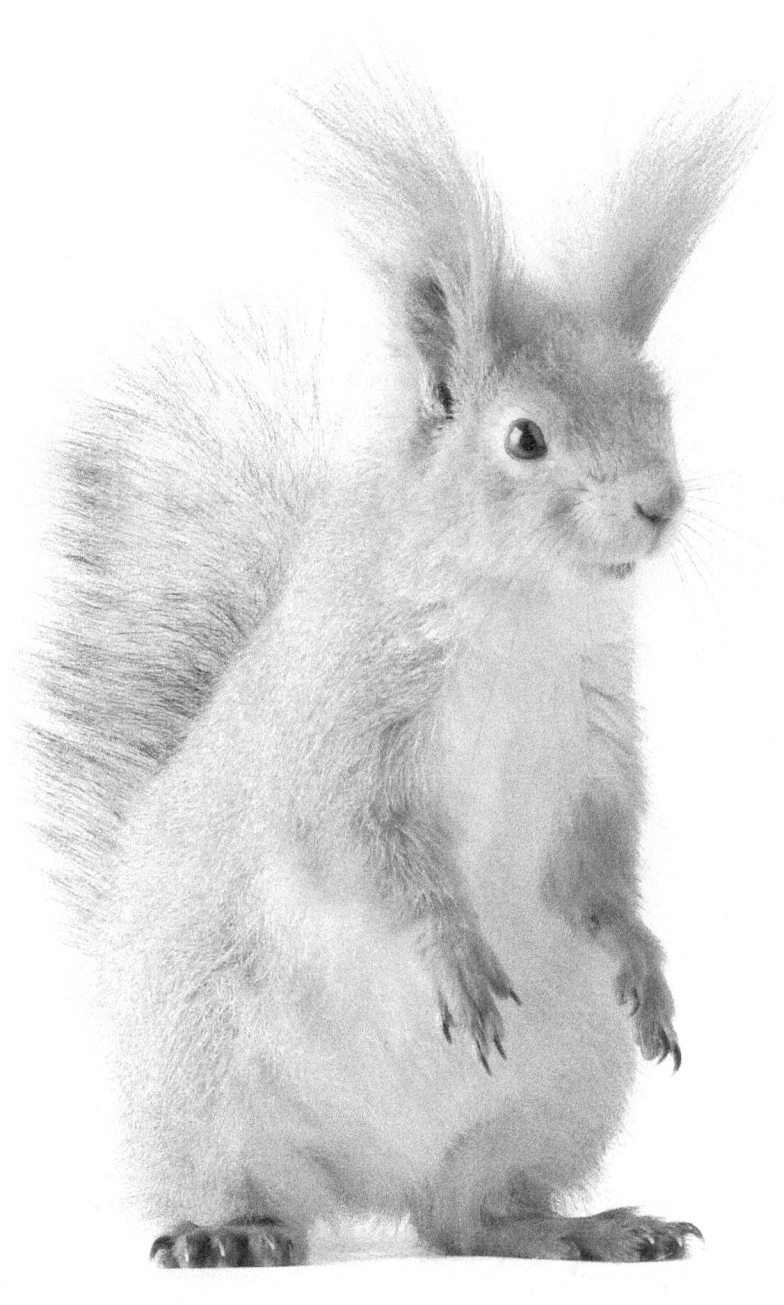

Draw the Eiffel Tower for this French poodle to admire.

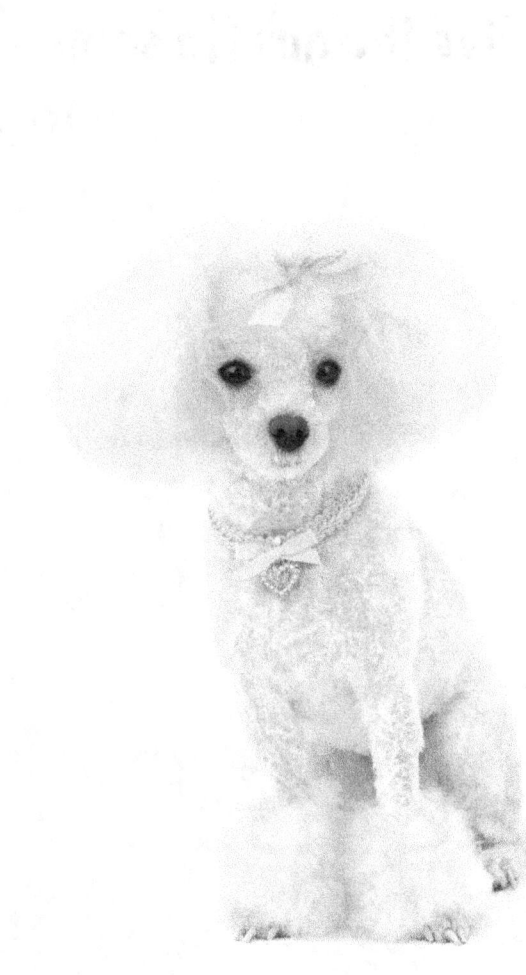

Give the giraffe some water skis and then draw a boat to pull it along.

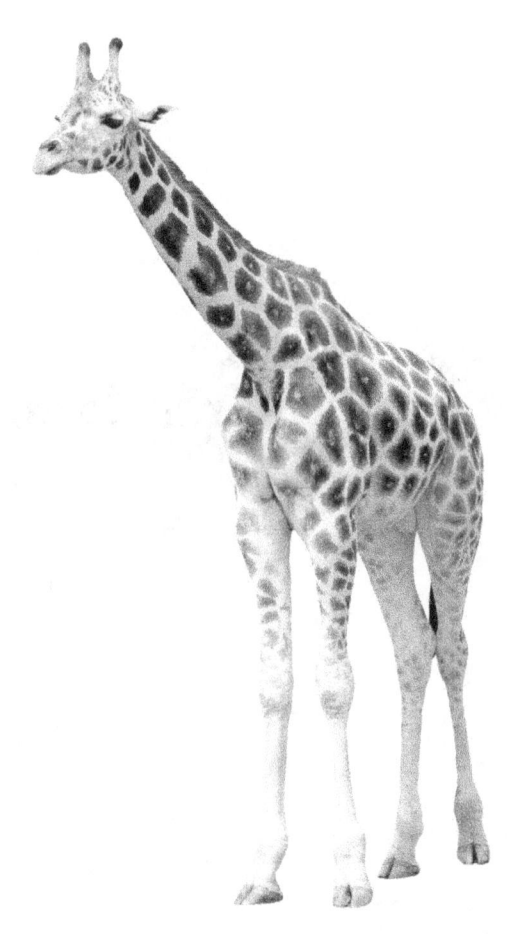

Transform this turtle in to a ninja.

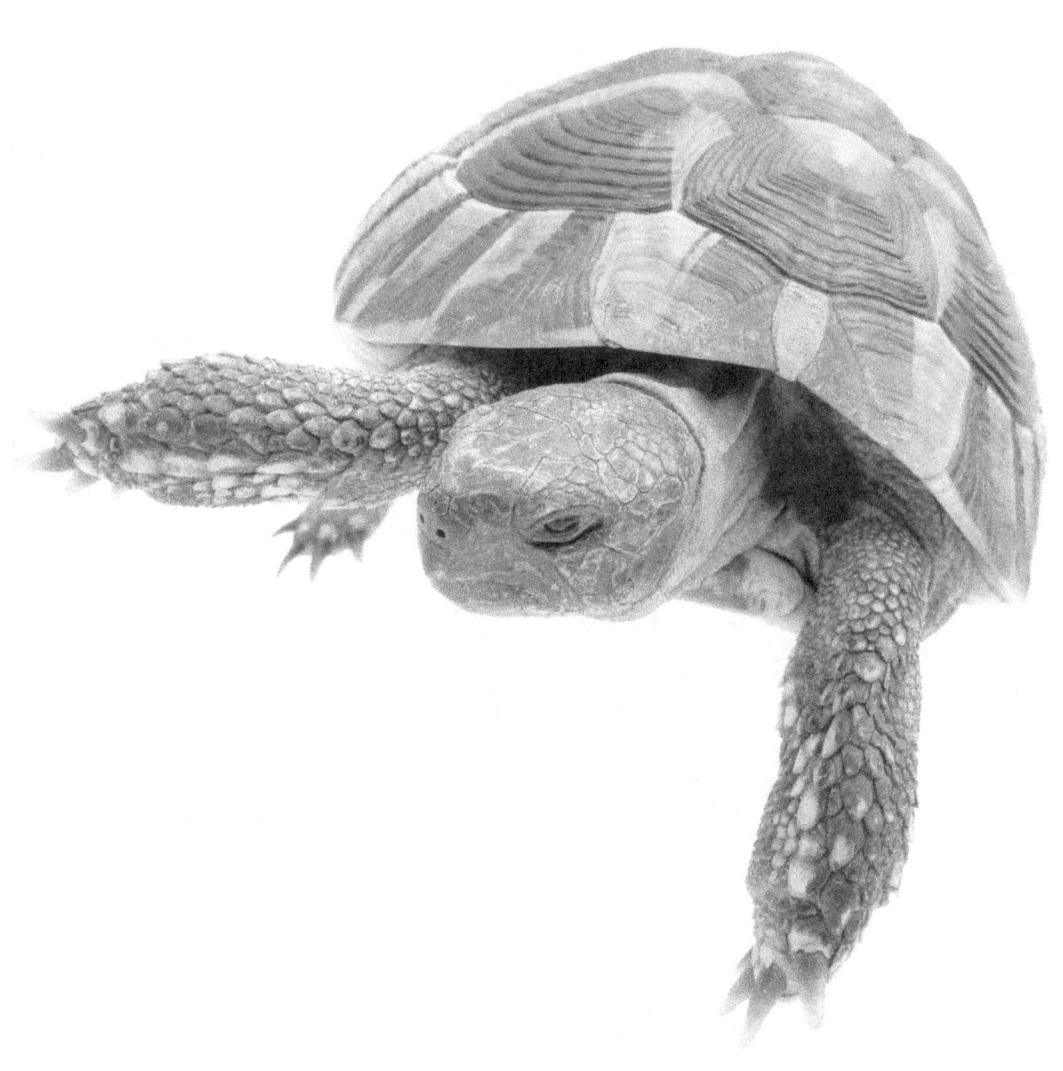

Dress this bear in Bavarian clothes and then give it a pretzel to munch.

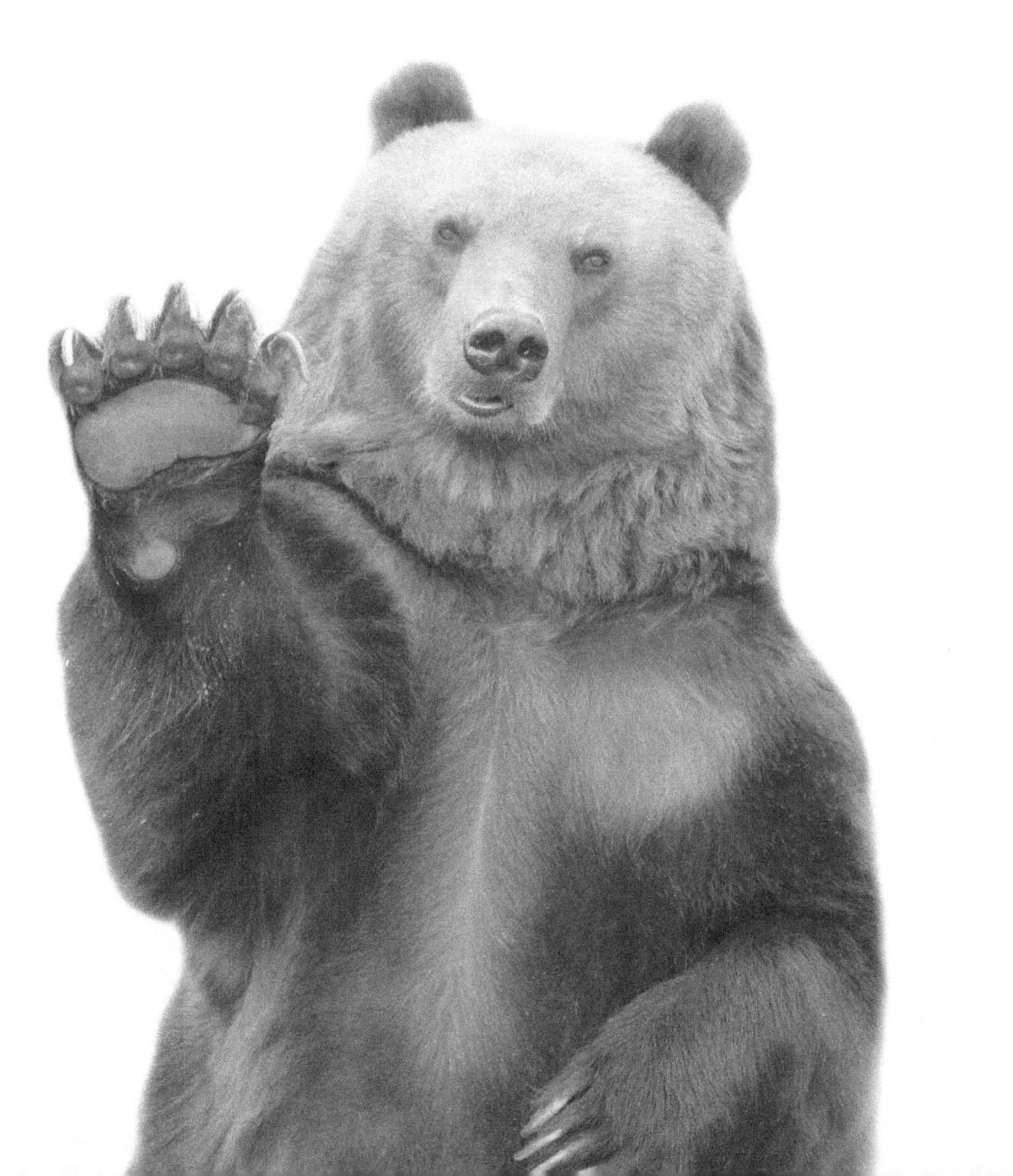

Draw some potatoes lounging on the couch.

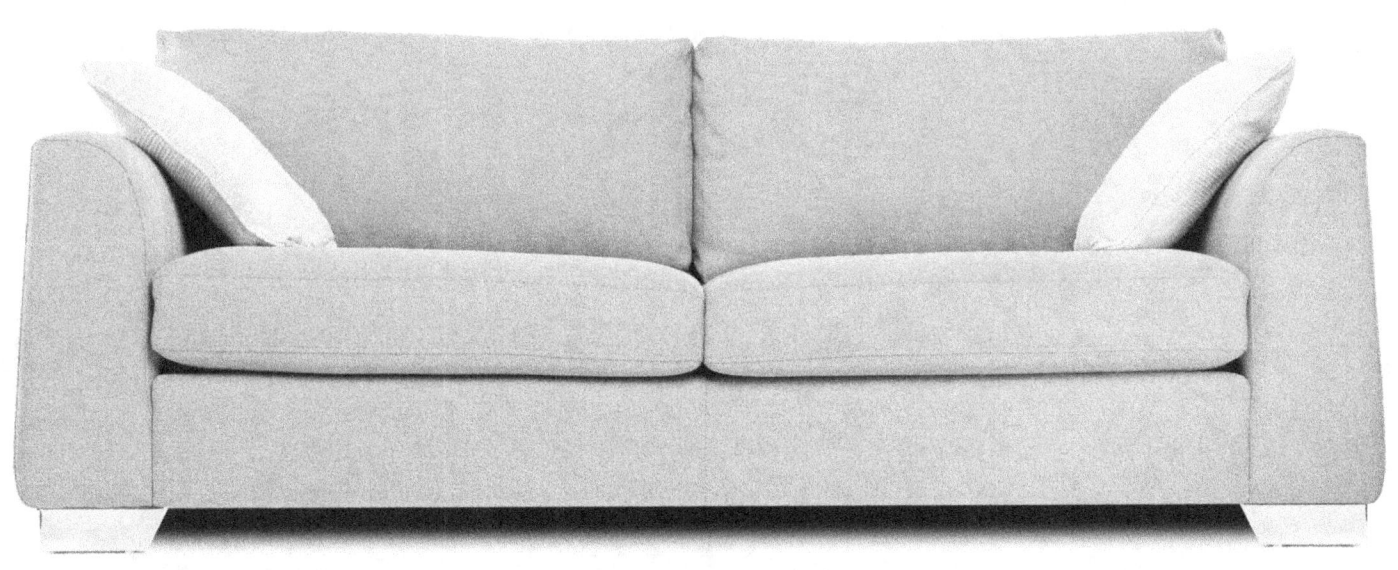

Draw a school of fish riding on the bus.

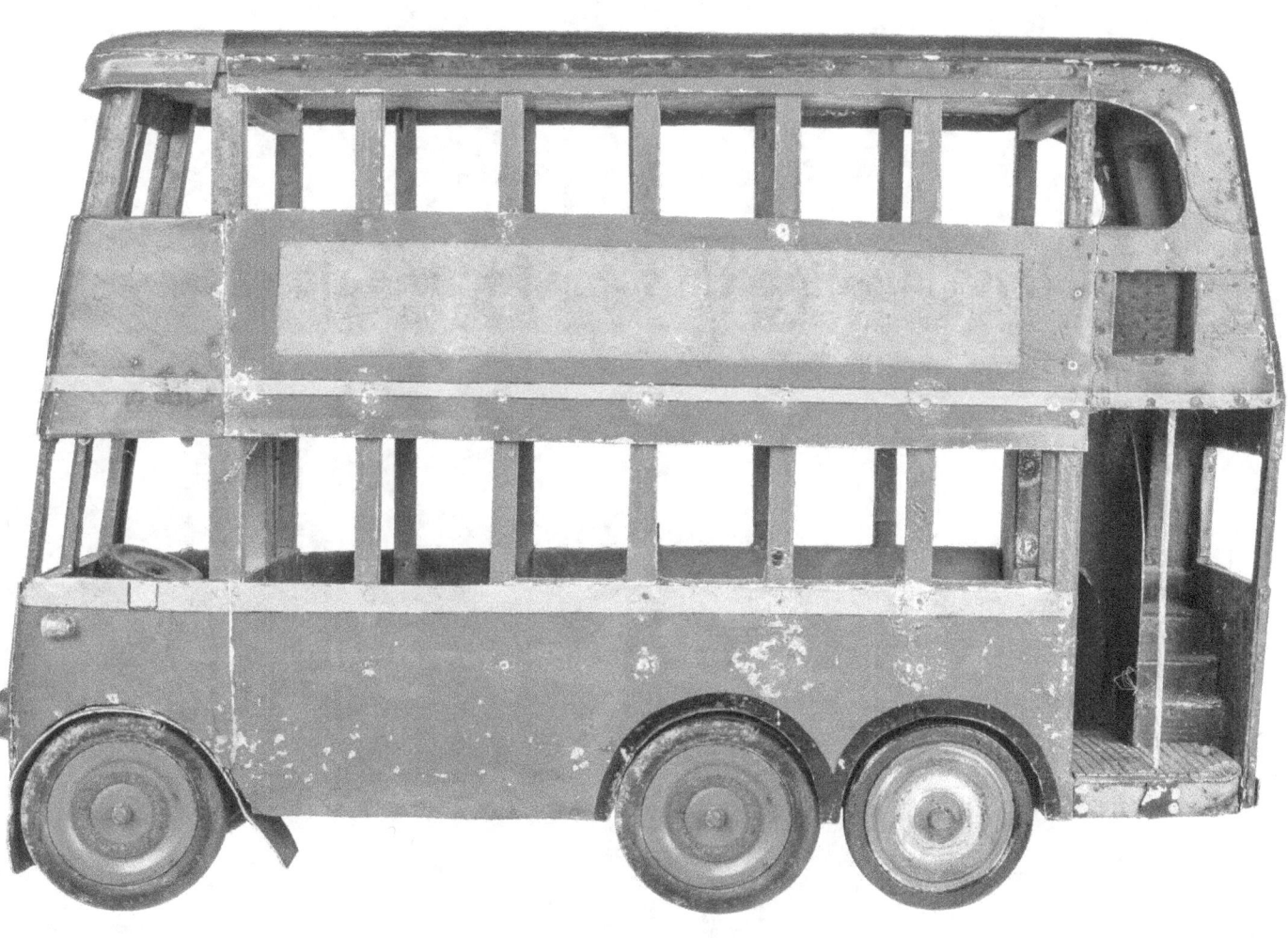

Dress this hippo in some footie pajamas.

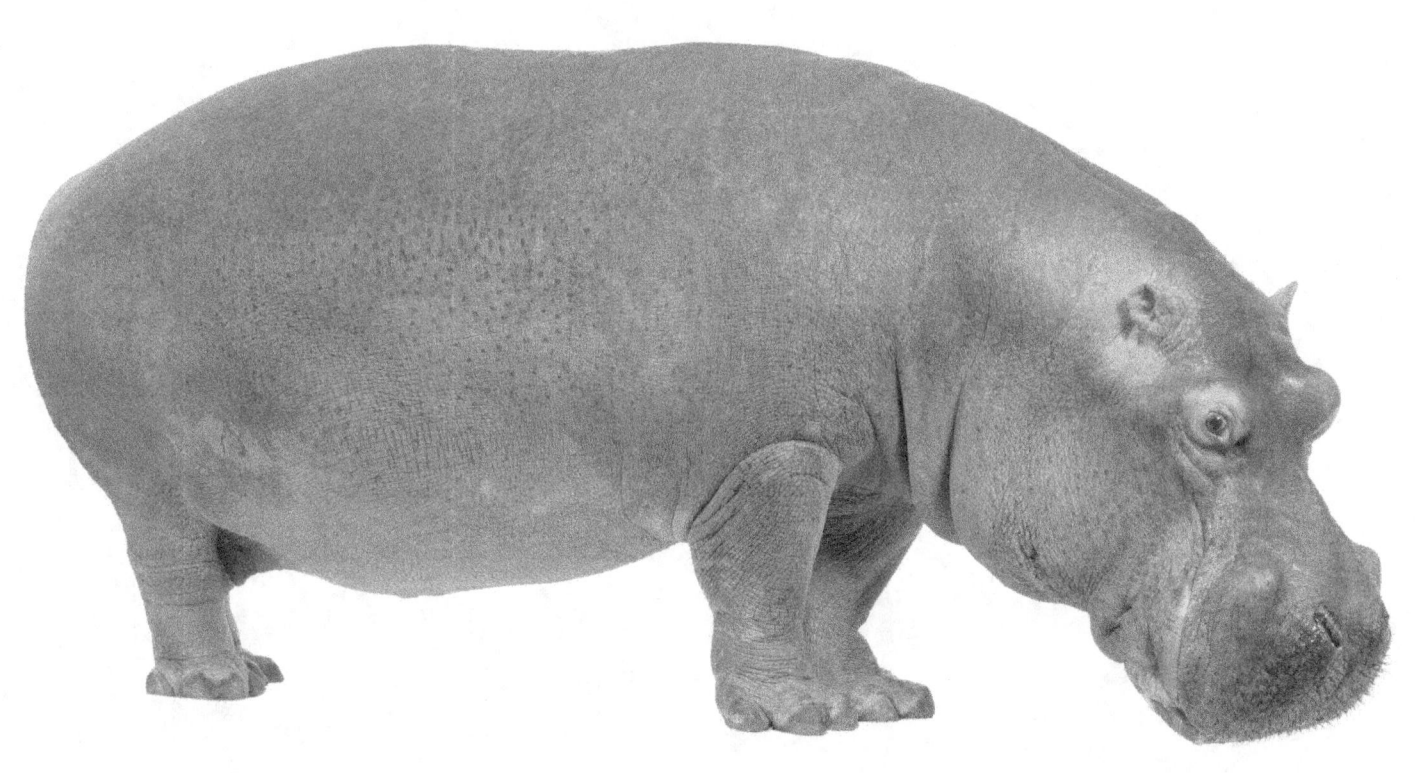

Give the llama a fedora and a mustache.

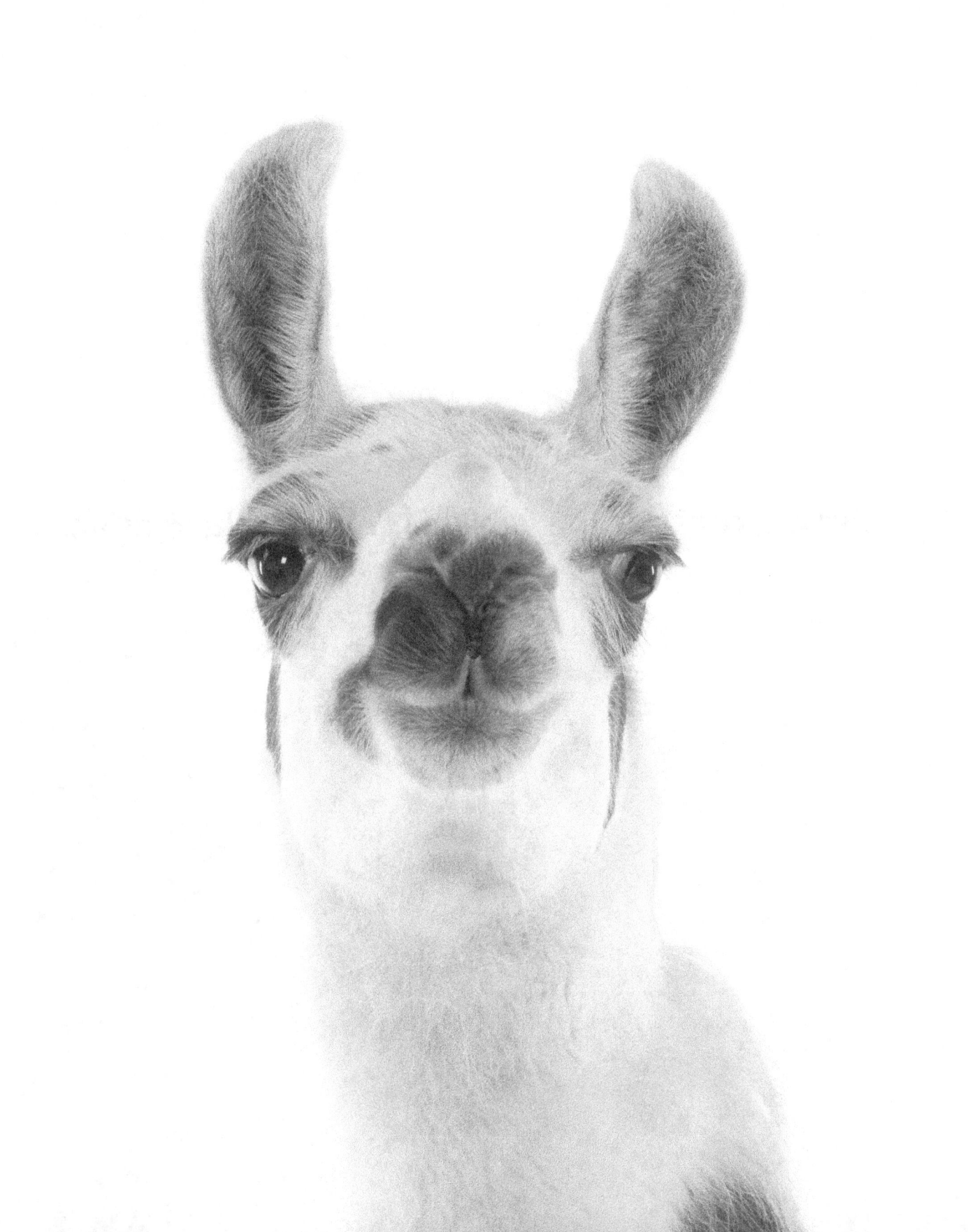

Draw a construction vehicle for the koala to drive.

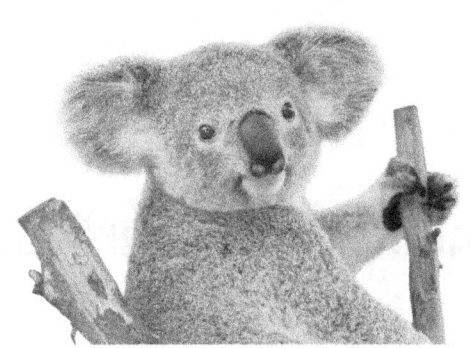

Draw a seal balancing the Earth on its nose.

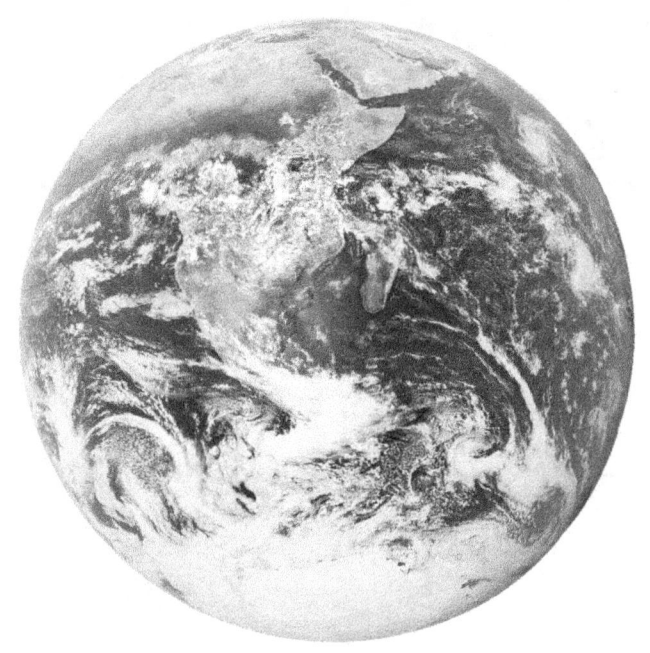

Draw some kangaroos jumping on the trampoline.

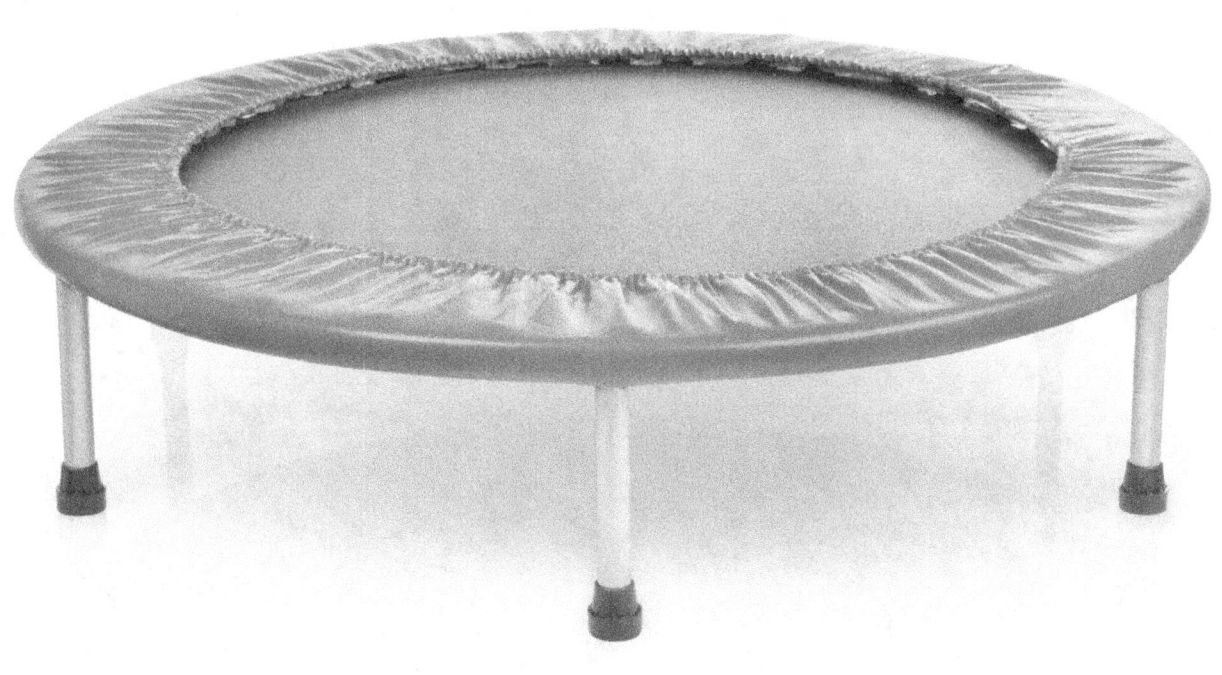

Turn these bunnies in to a couple basketball players.

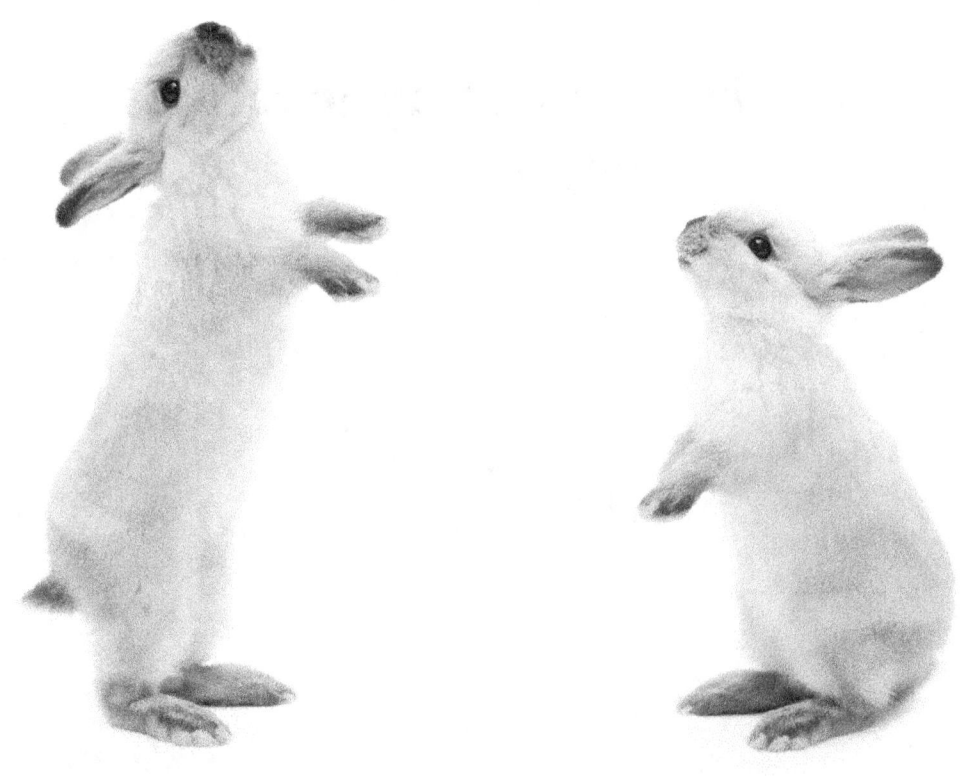

Transform this cat in to a DJ spinning records on a turntable.

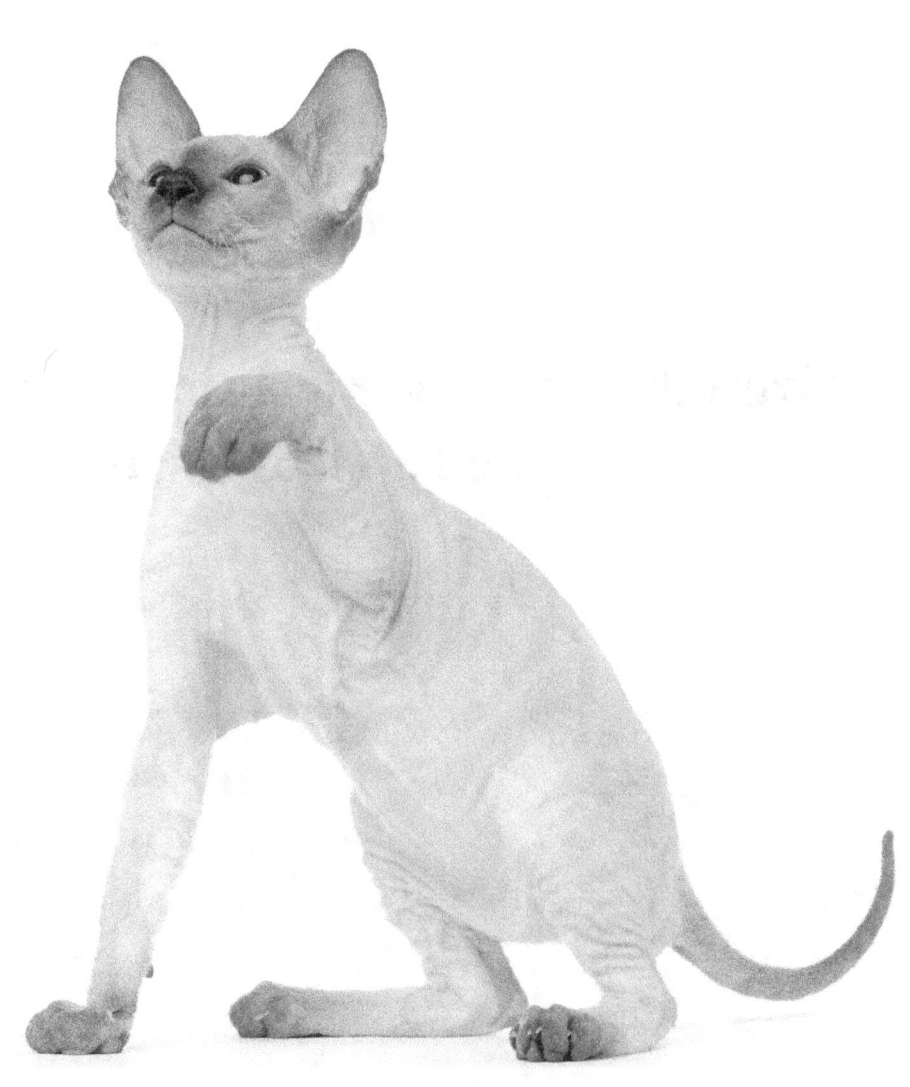

Dress this polar bear in a stocking hat, a scarf, and a set of mittens.

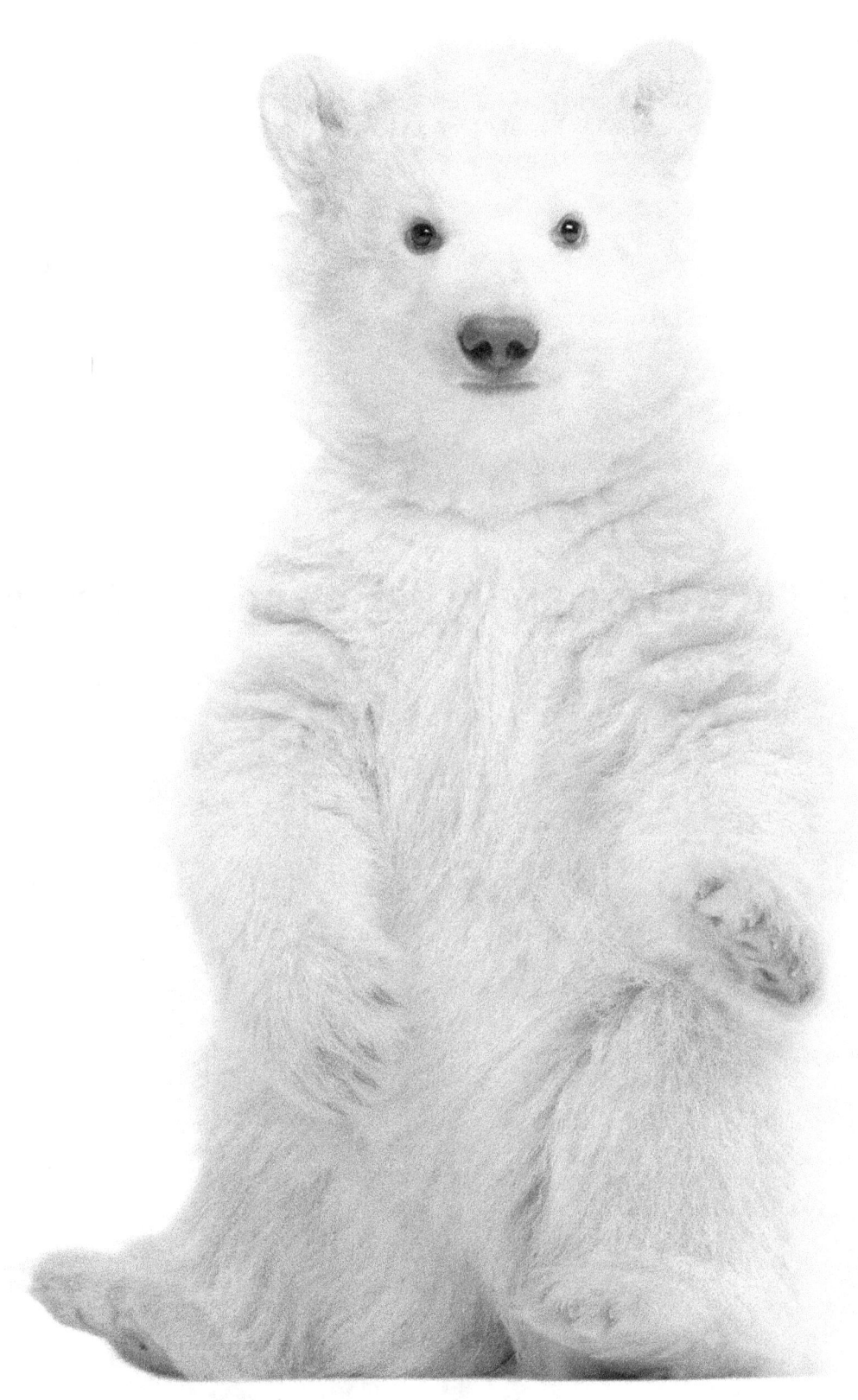

Give this little critter a pretty purse and a matching hat.

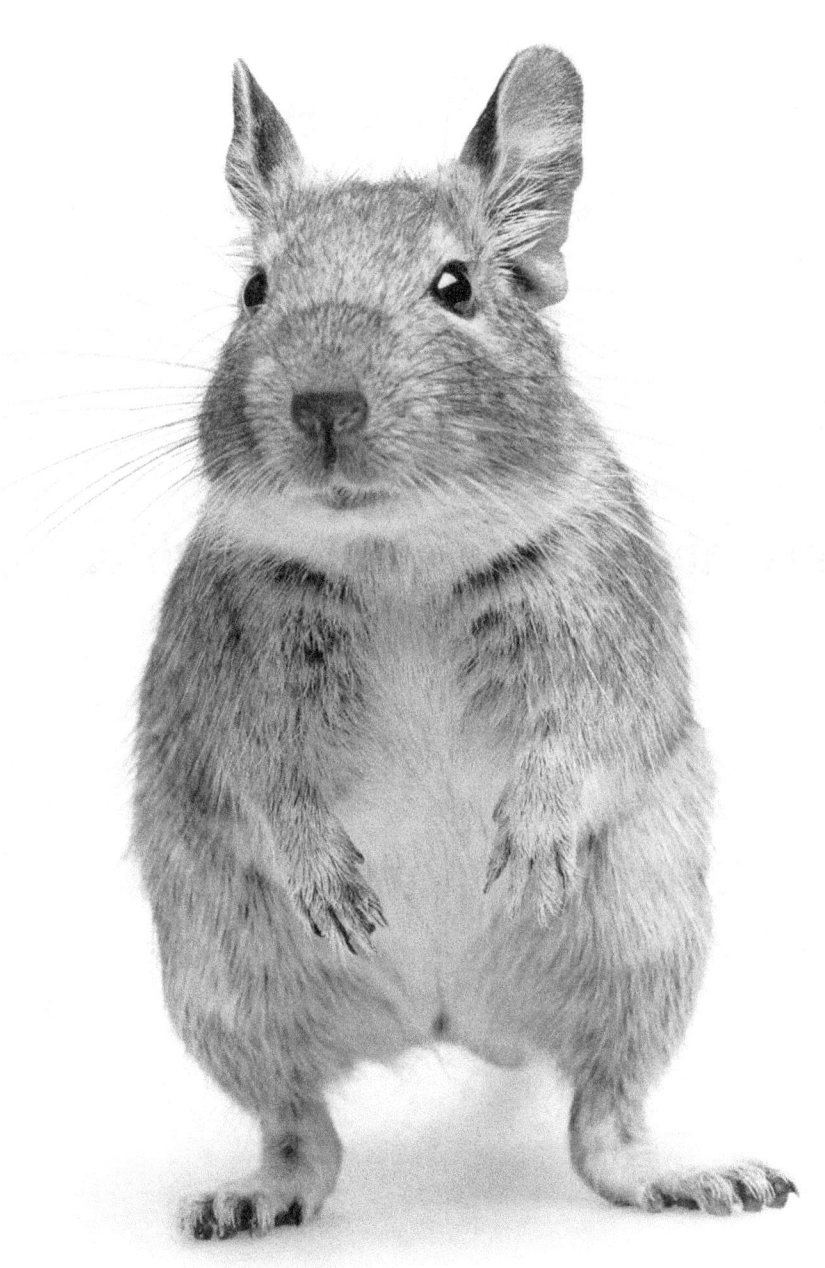

Turn this rabbit in to a magician who is pulling a human out of his hat.

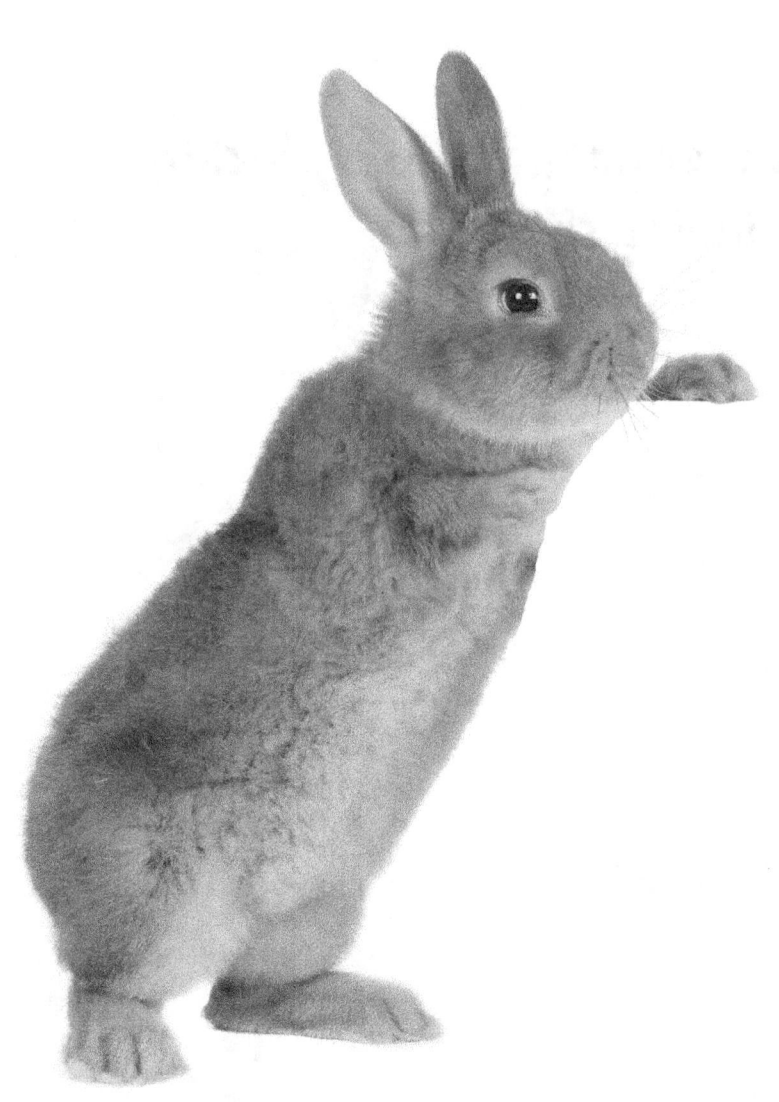

Turn this cat in to a soccer goalie who is blocking the winning shot.

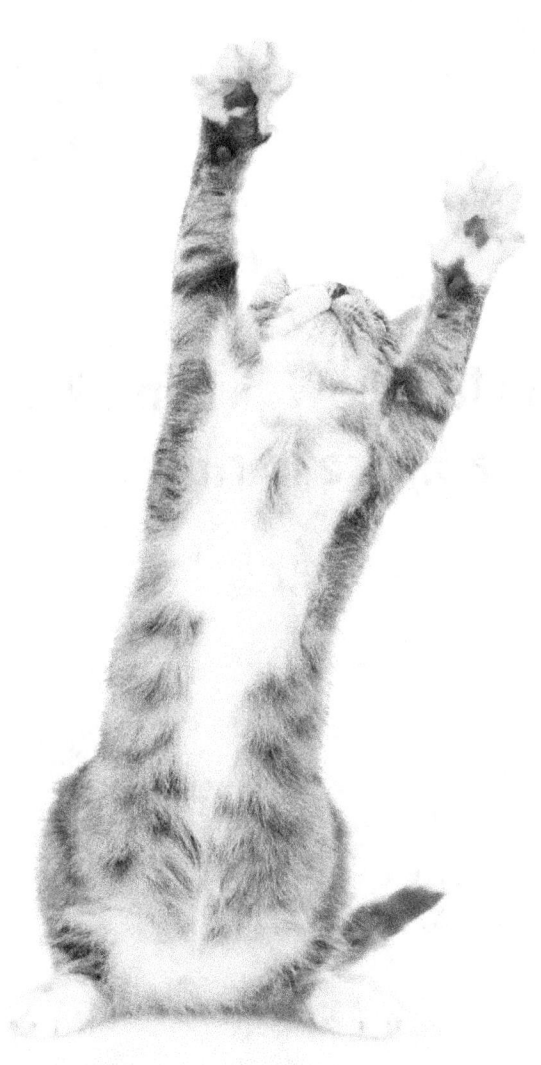

Turn this dog in to a cowgirl and then give her
a horse to ride.

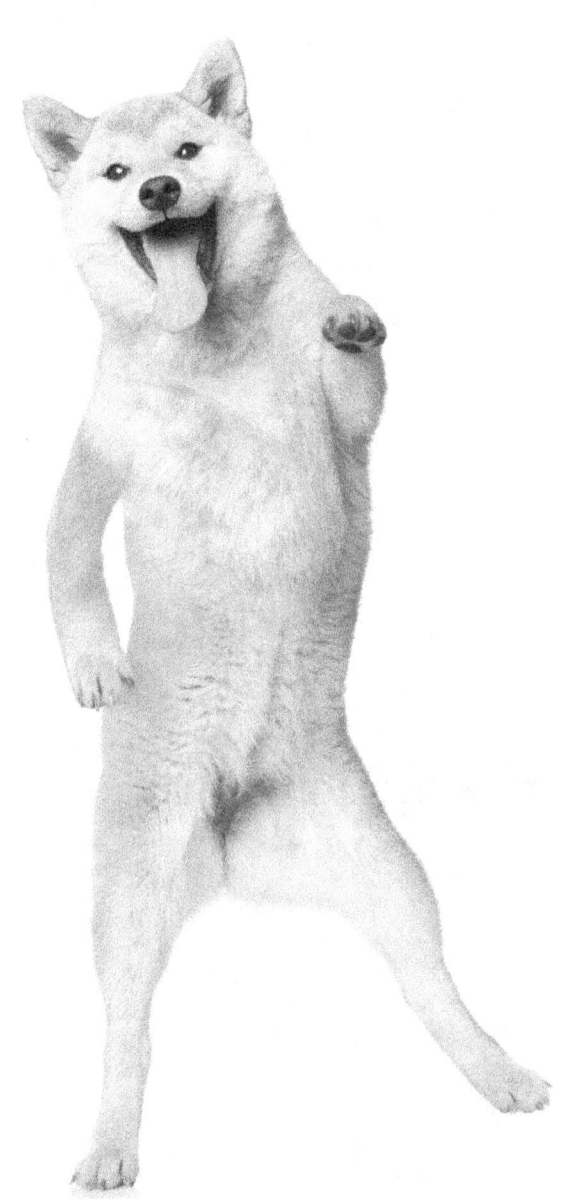

Draw a mohawk on the fox.

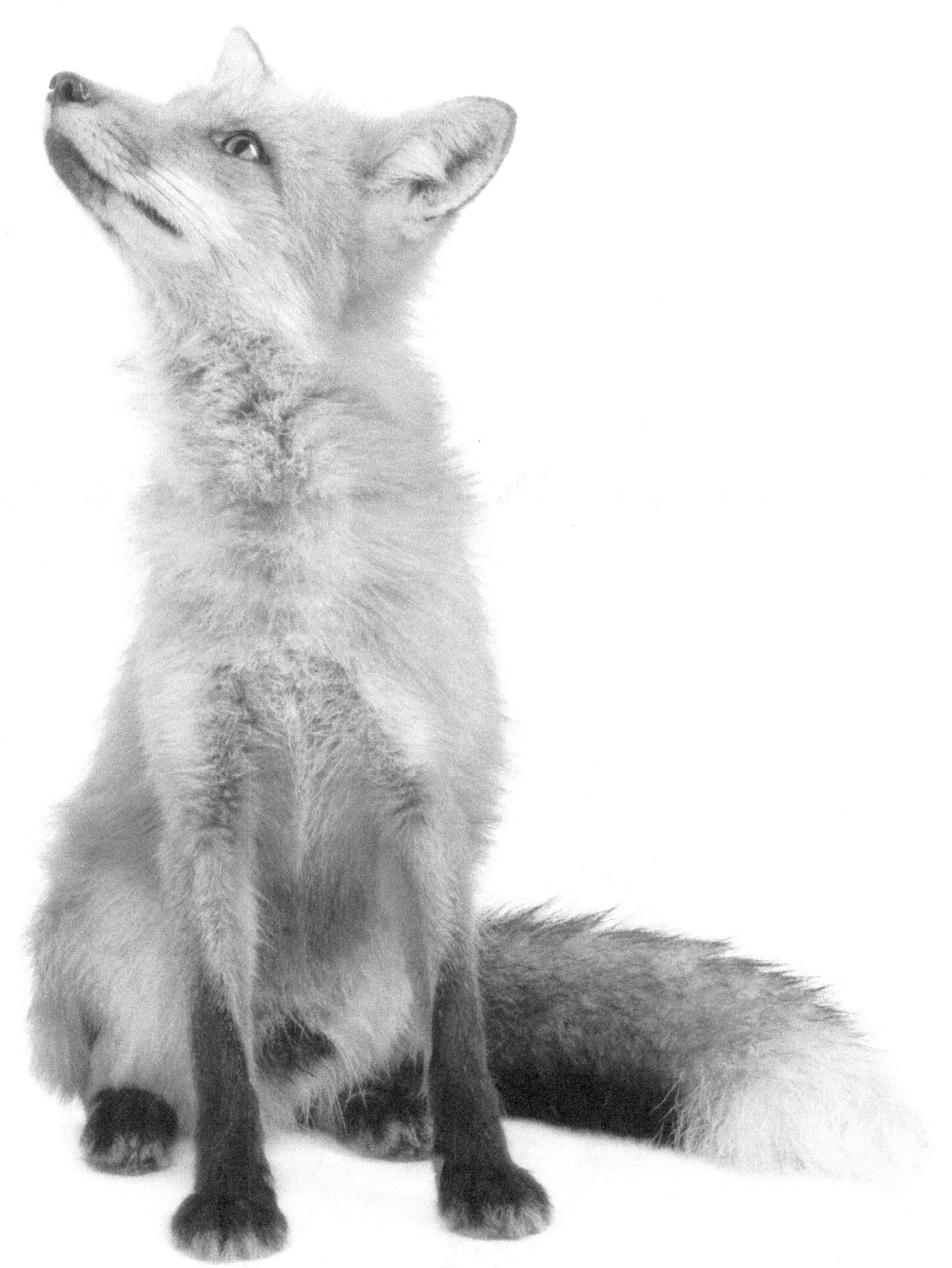

Finish creating Edvard Munch's masterpiece *The Scream*.

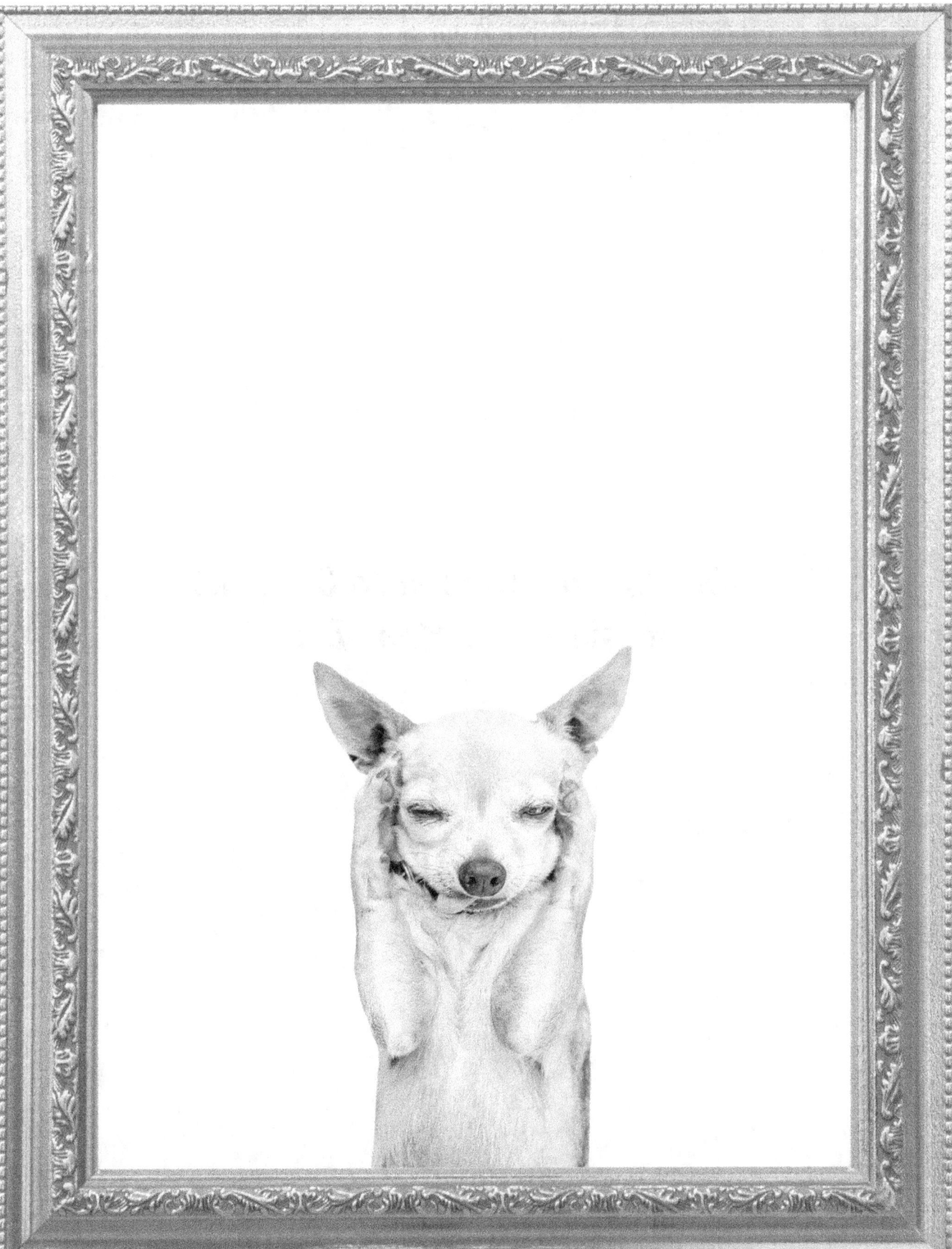

Finish creating Leonardo Da Vinci's masterpiece *Mona Lisa*.

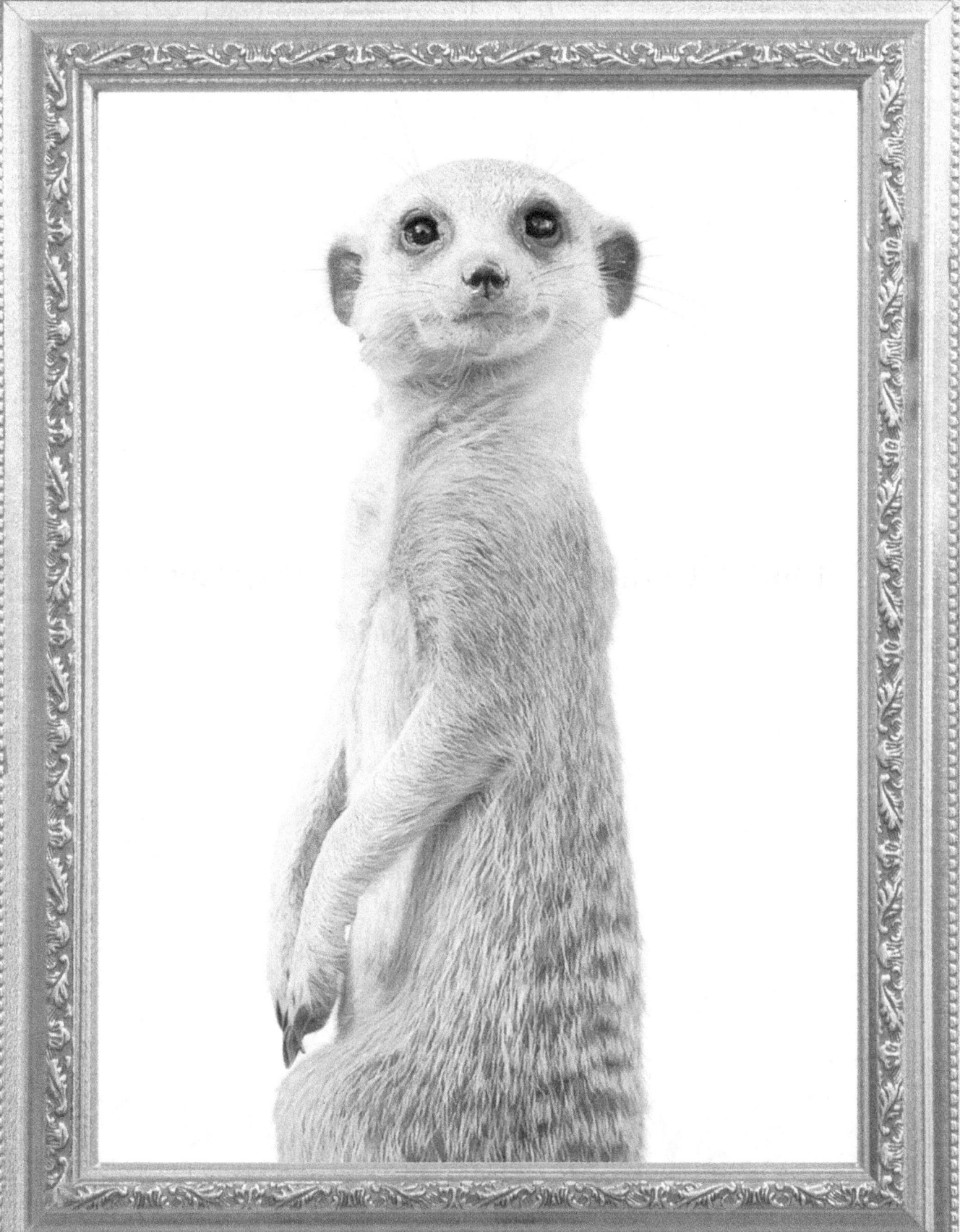

Finish creating Grant Wood's masterpiece *American Gothic.*

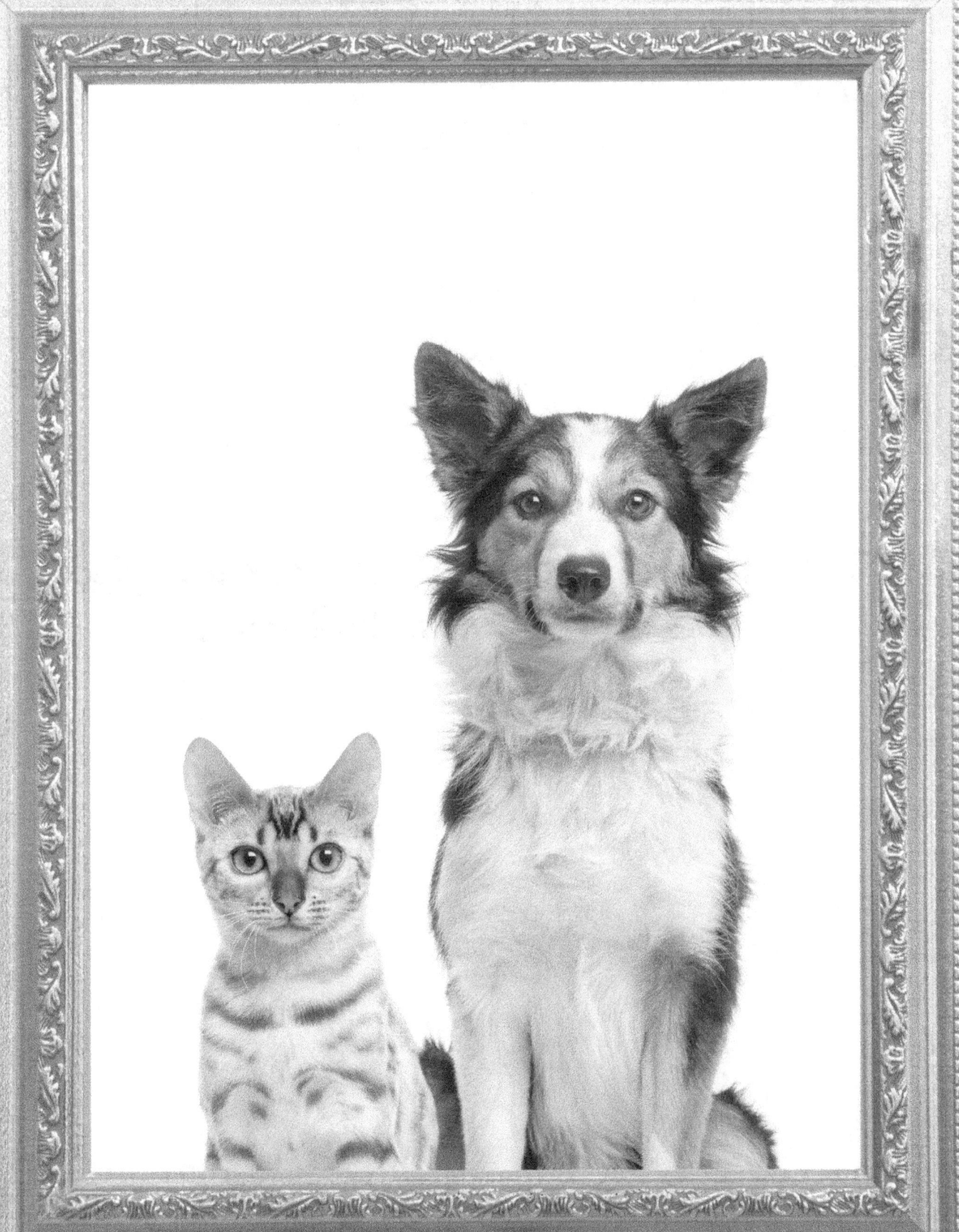

Finish creating Johannes Vermeer's masterpiece *The Girl With The Pearl Earring*.

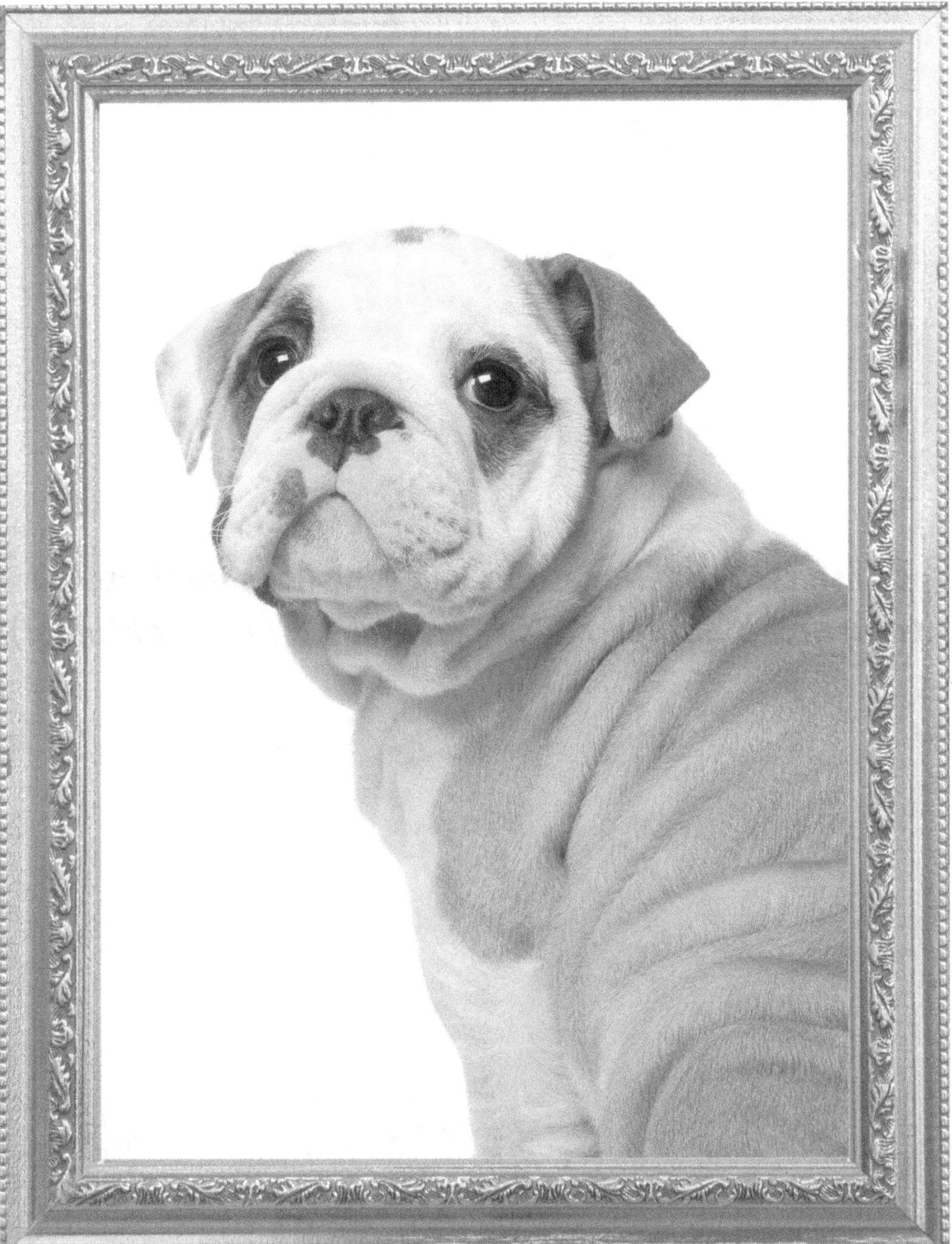

Finish creating James McNeill Whistler's masterpiece *Grey and Black No.1* (also known as *Whistler's Mother*).

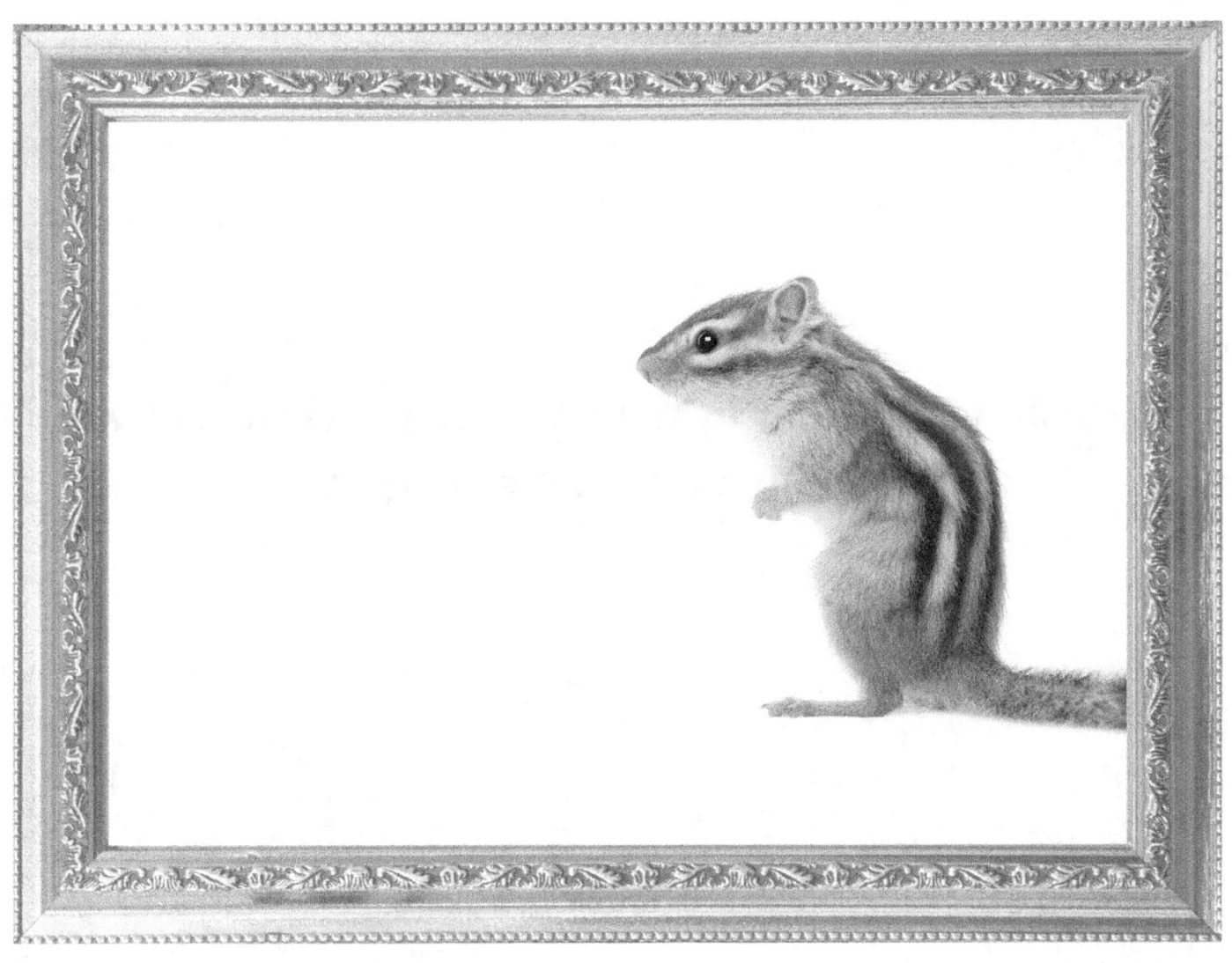

Turn these penguins in to a construction crew who are working on building an igloo.

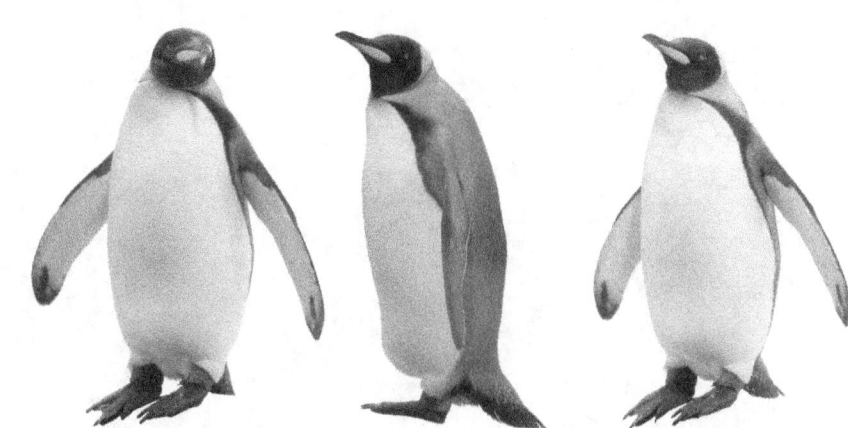

Transform this cat in to a super hero who is flying over the city.

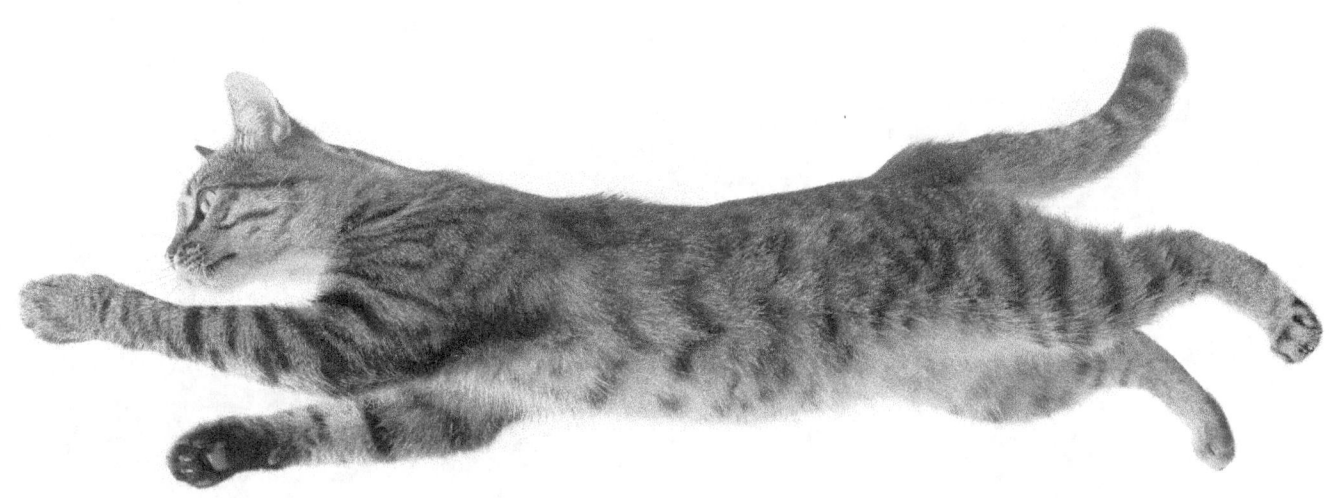

Turn this monkey in to a clown.

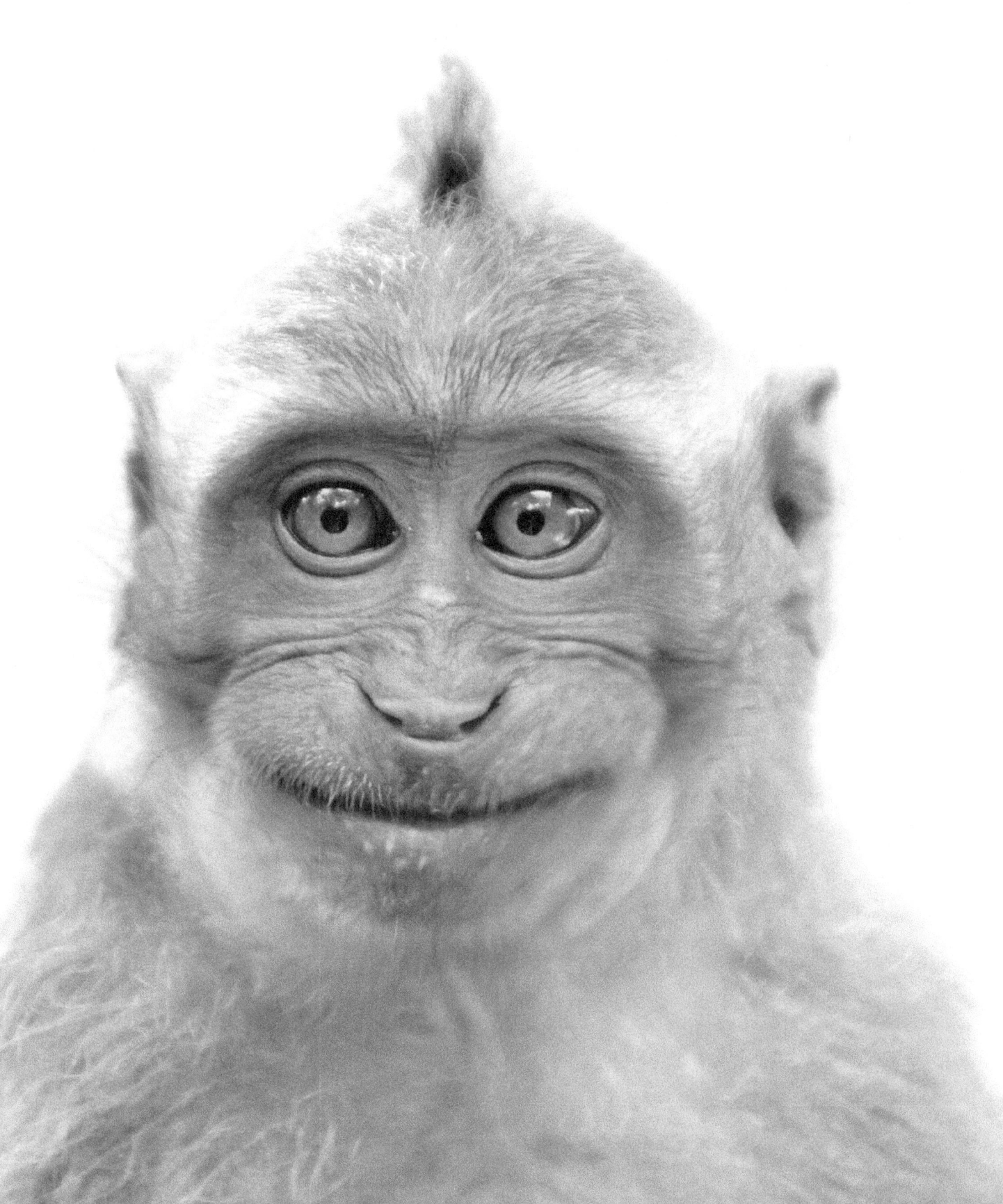

Draw a mermaid caught on the fisherman's line.

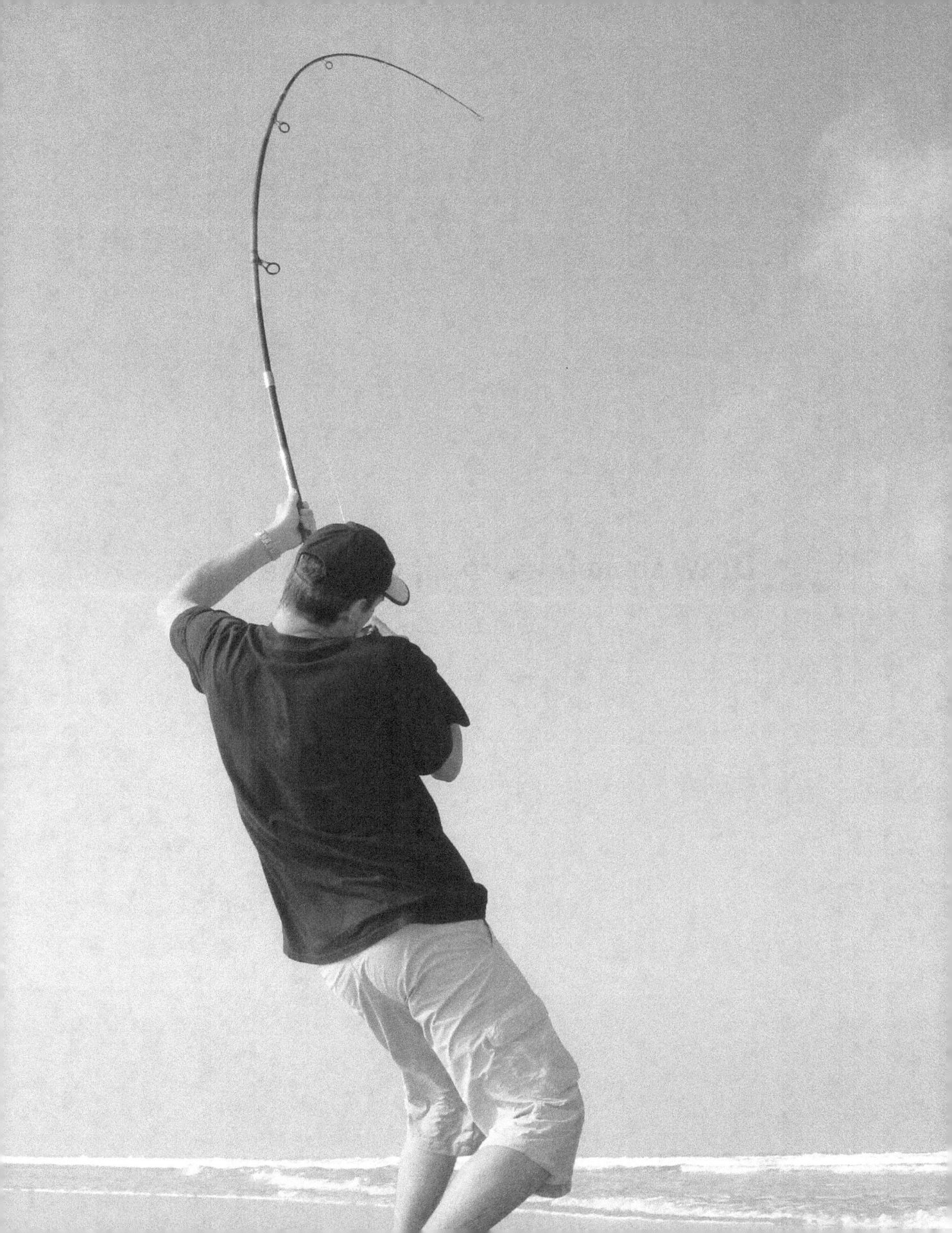

Draw some finger puppets on the hand.

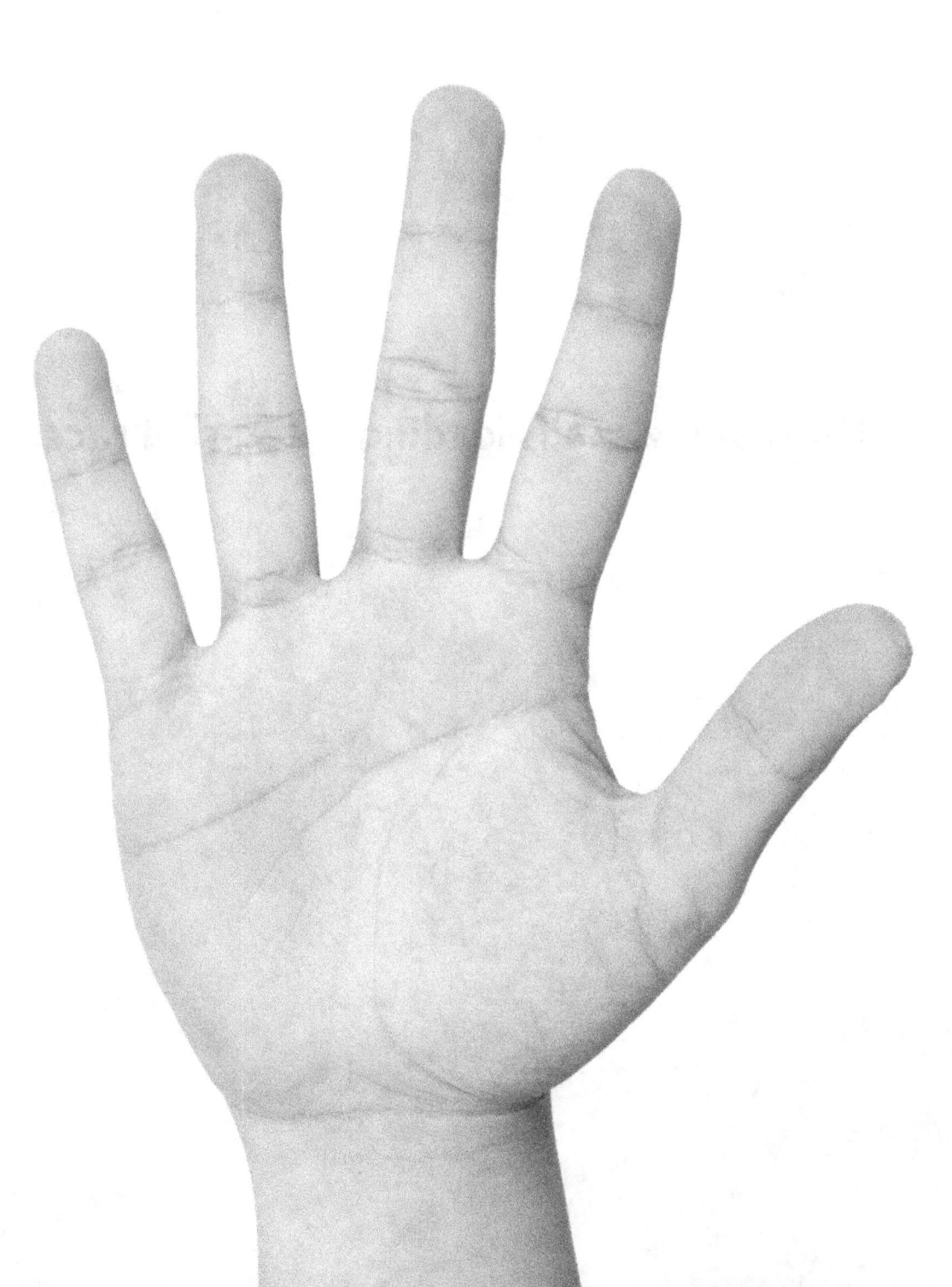

Draw some snails leading a dog sled race.

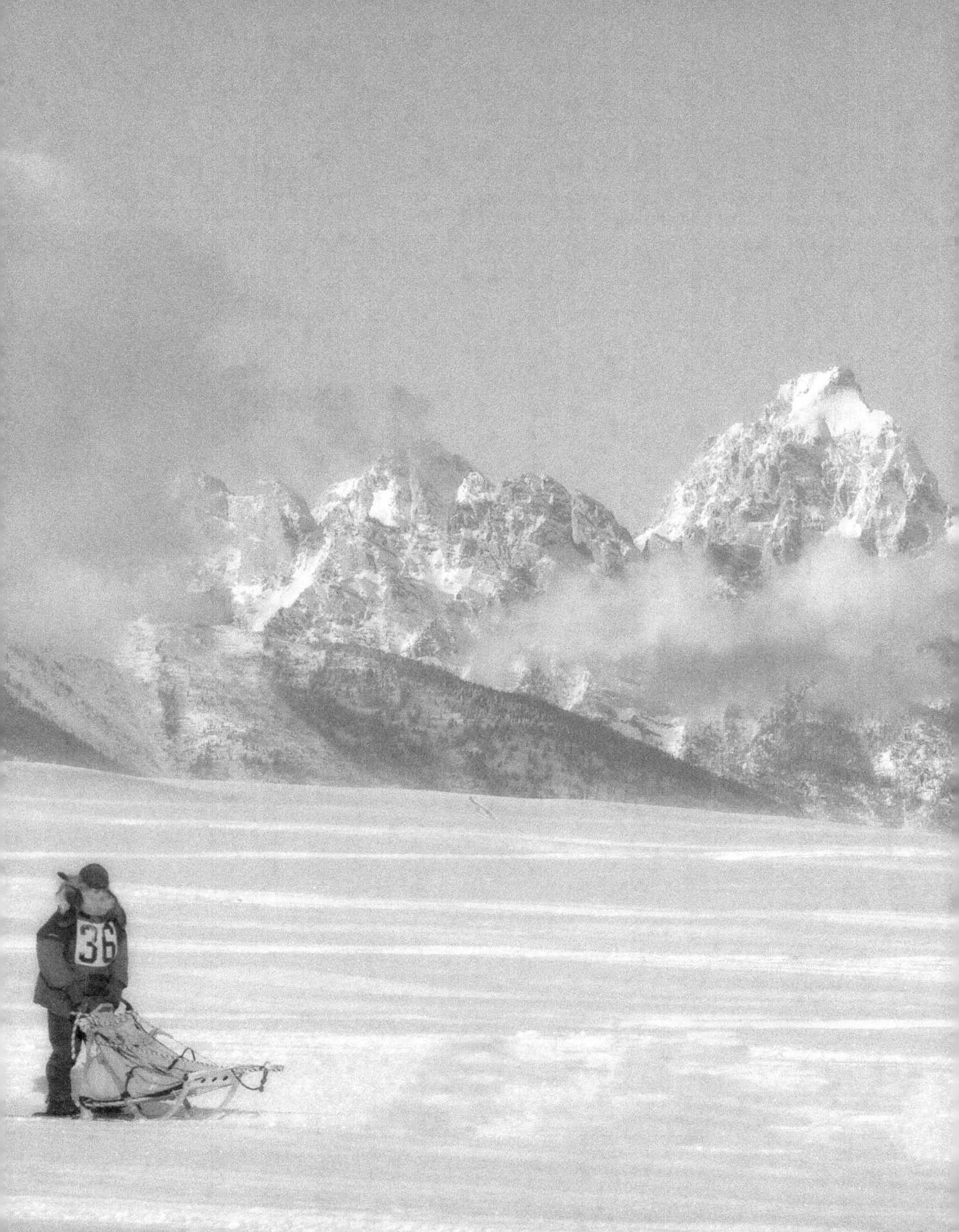

Draw a couple monsters riding on the subway.

Draw some astronaut mice who went to the moon because they thought that it was made of cheese.

Turn these cats in to two eager students.

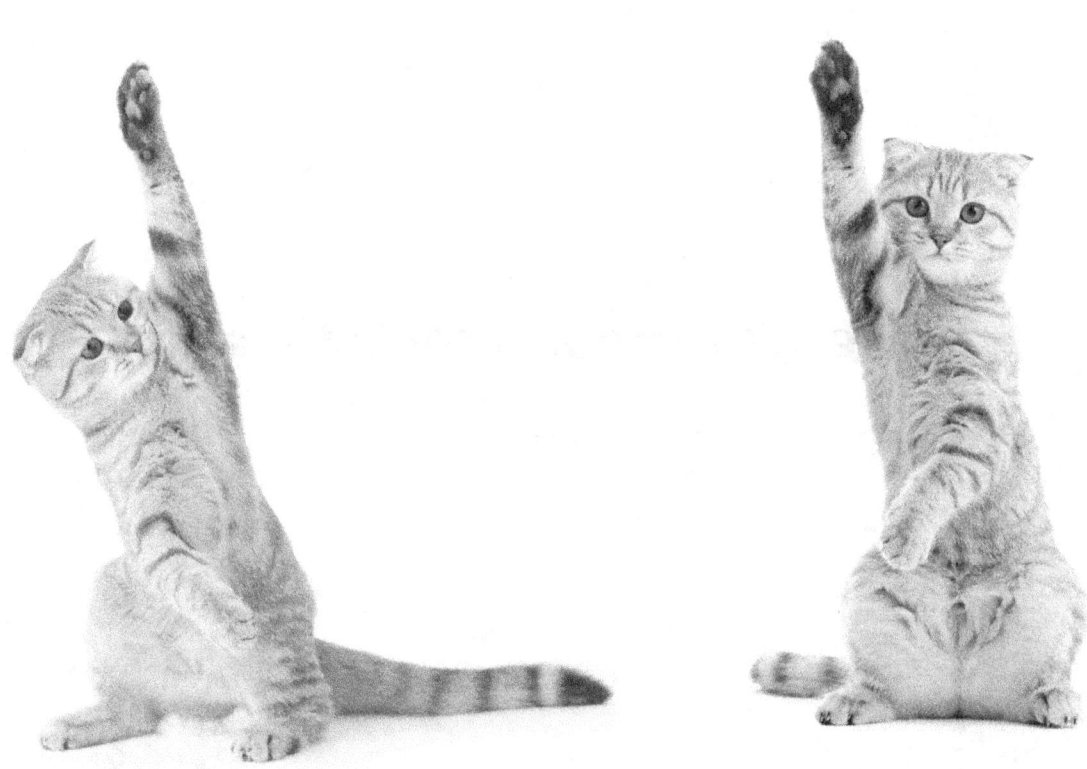

Give this raccoon a cookie to eat.

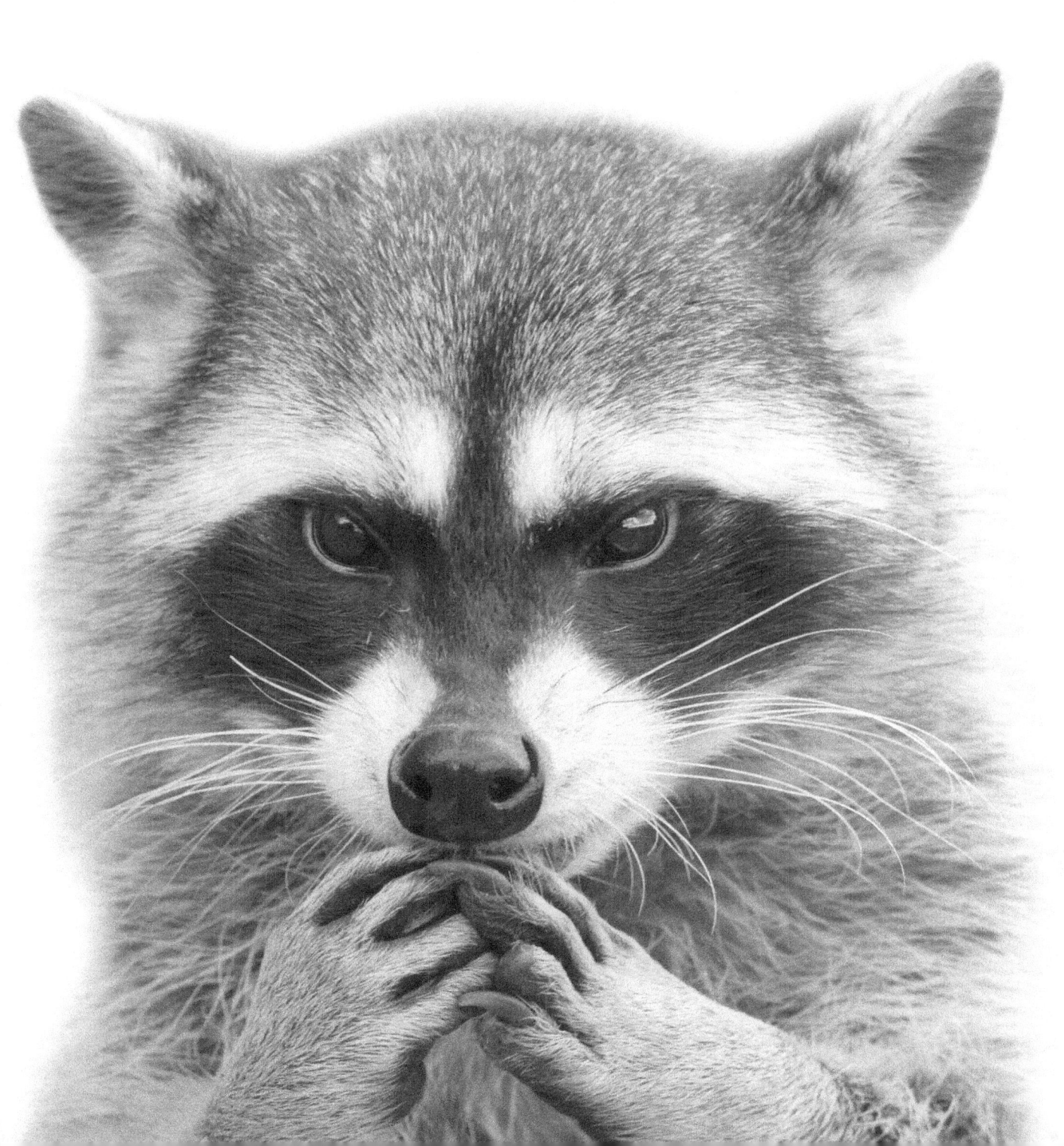

Give this goat a goatee and a funny hat.

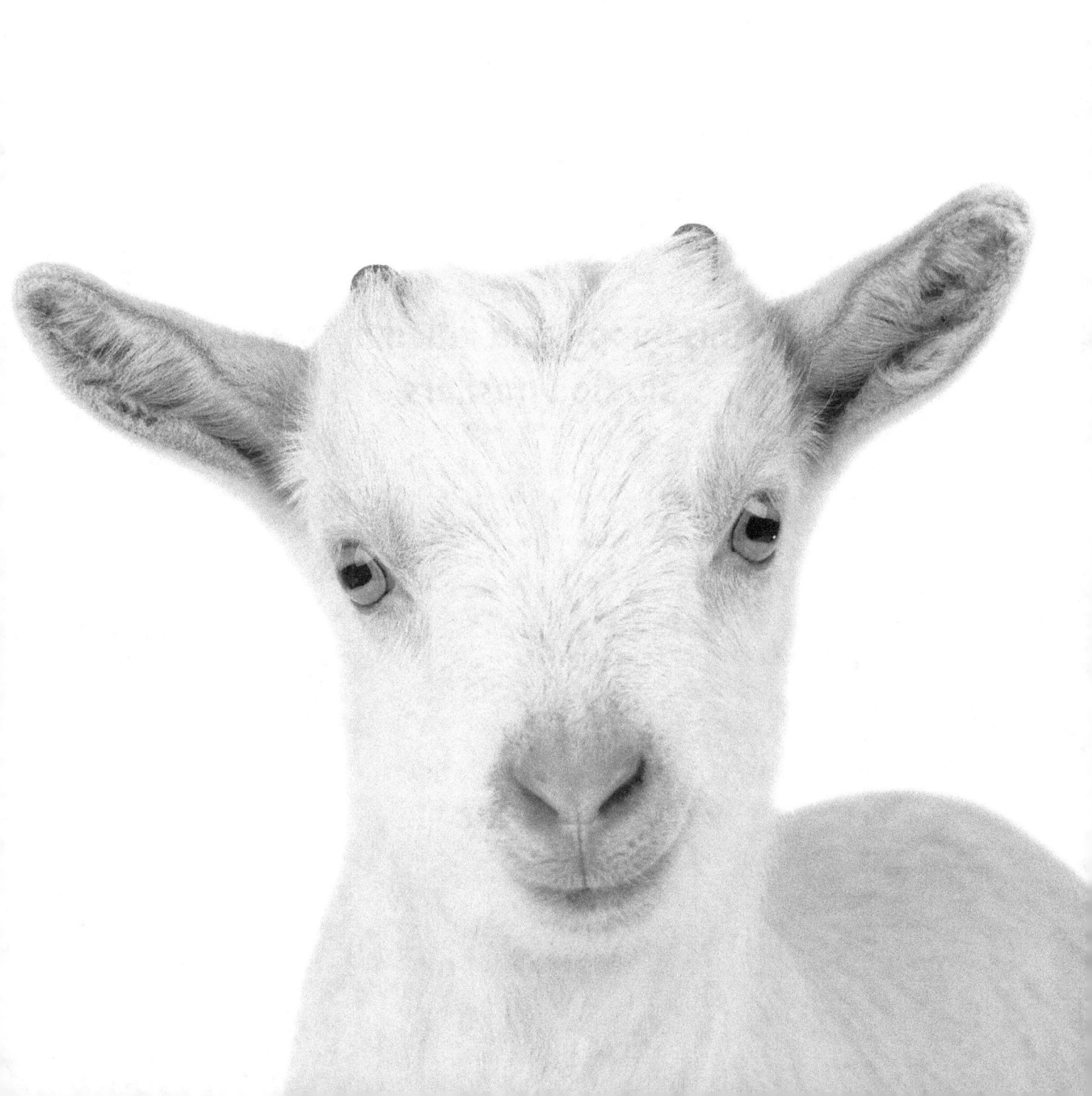

Transform this puppy and kitten in to a couple studio wrestlers.

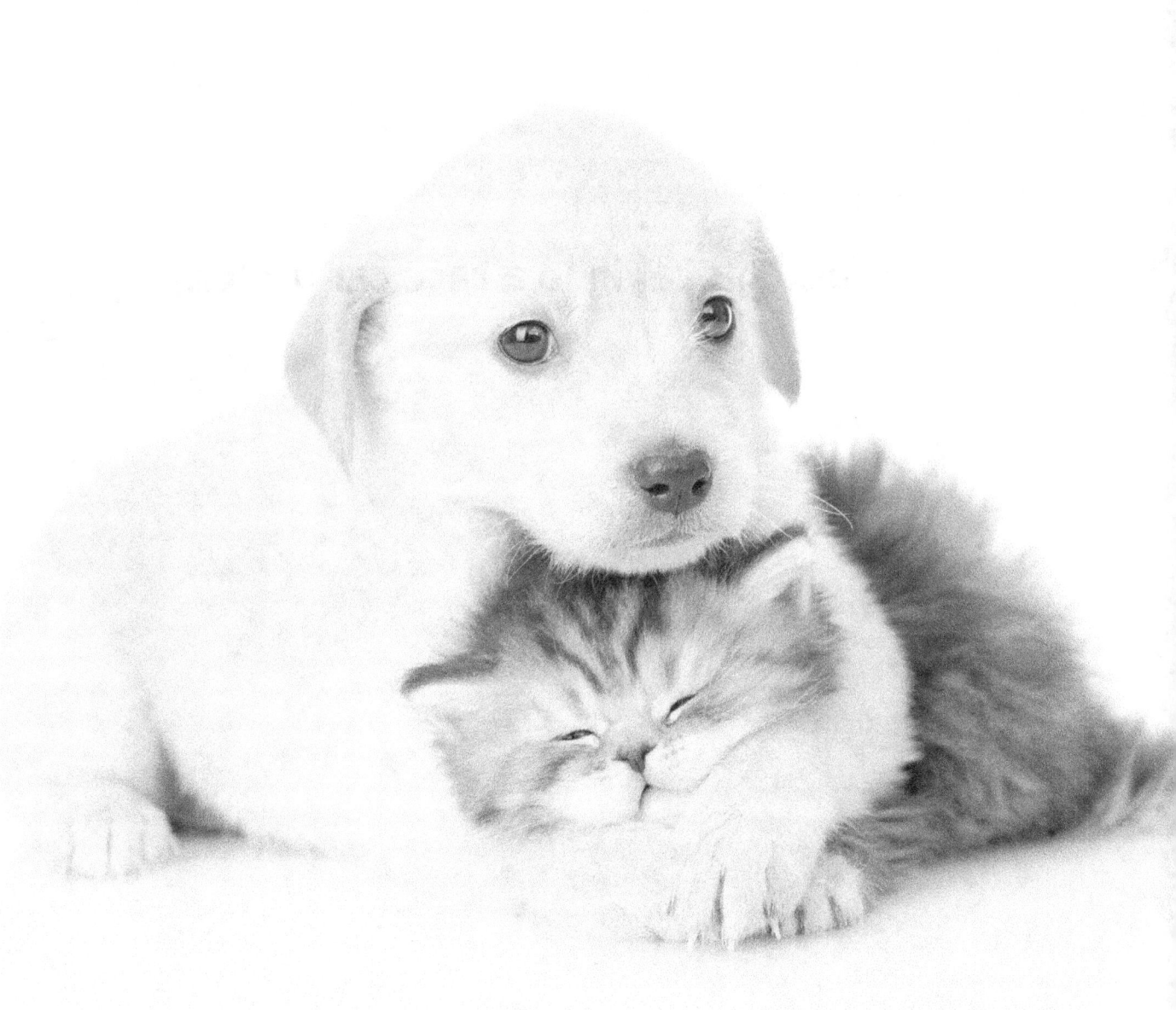

Turn this cat in to a race car driver.

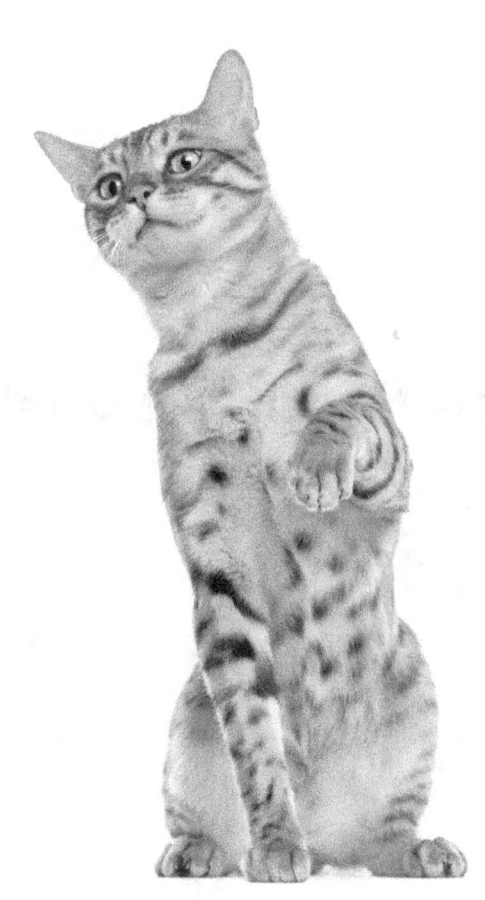

Give these French fries berets and funny faces.

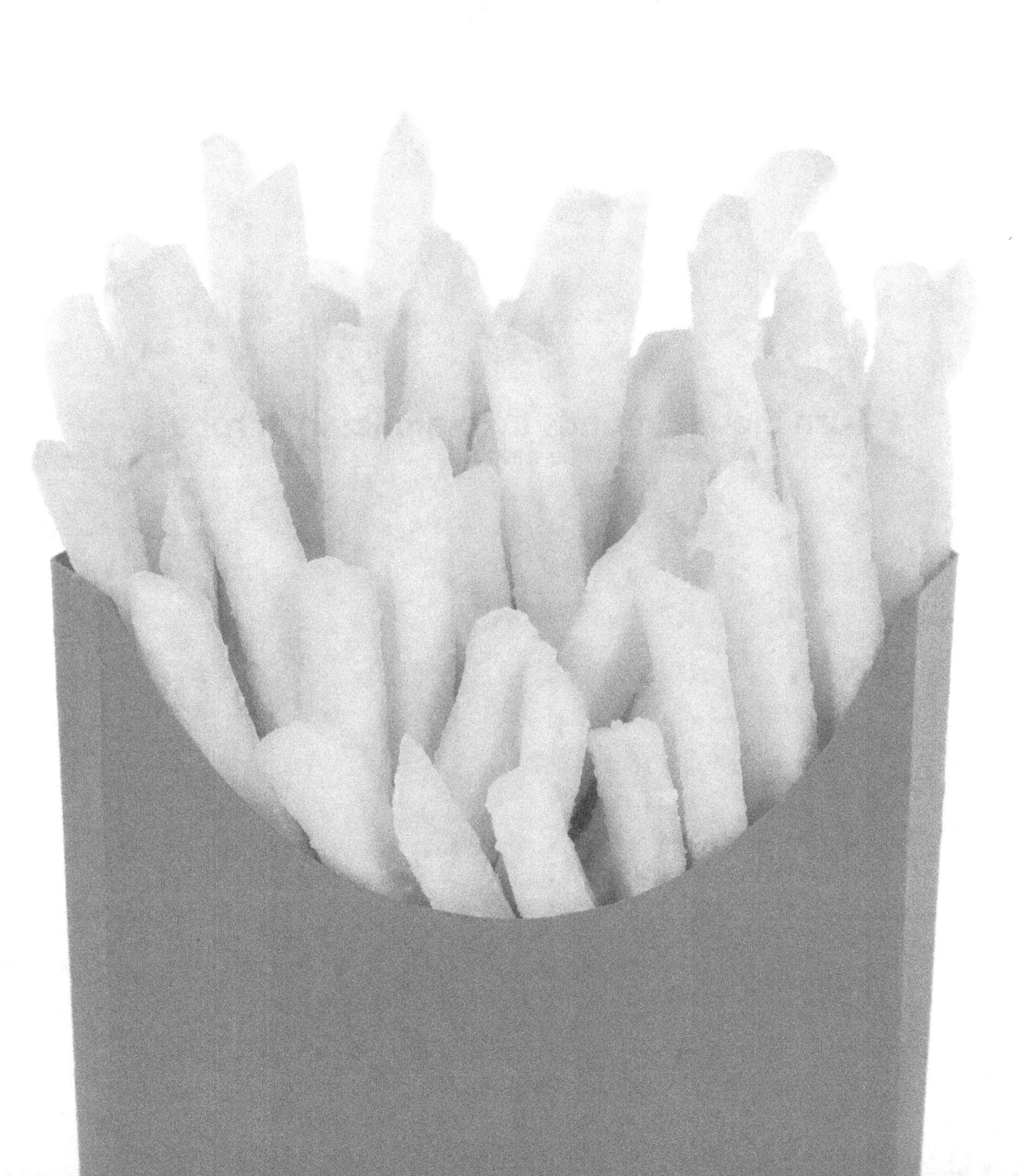

Turn these almonds in to amazing acrobats.

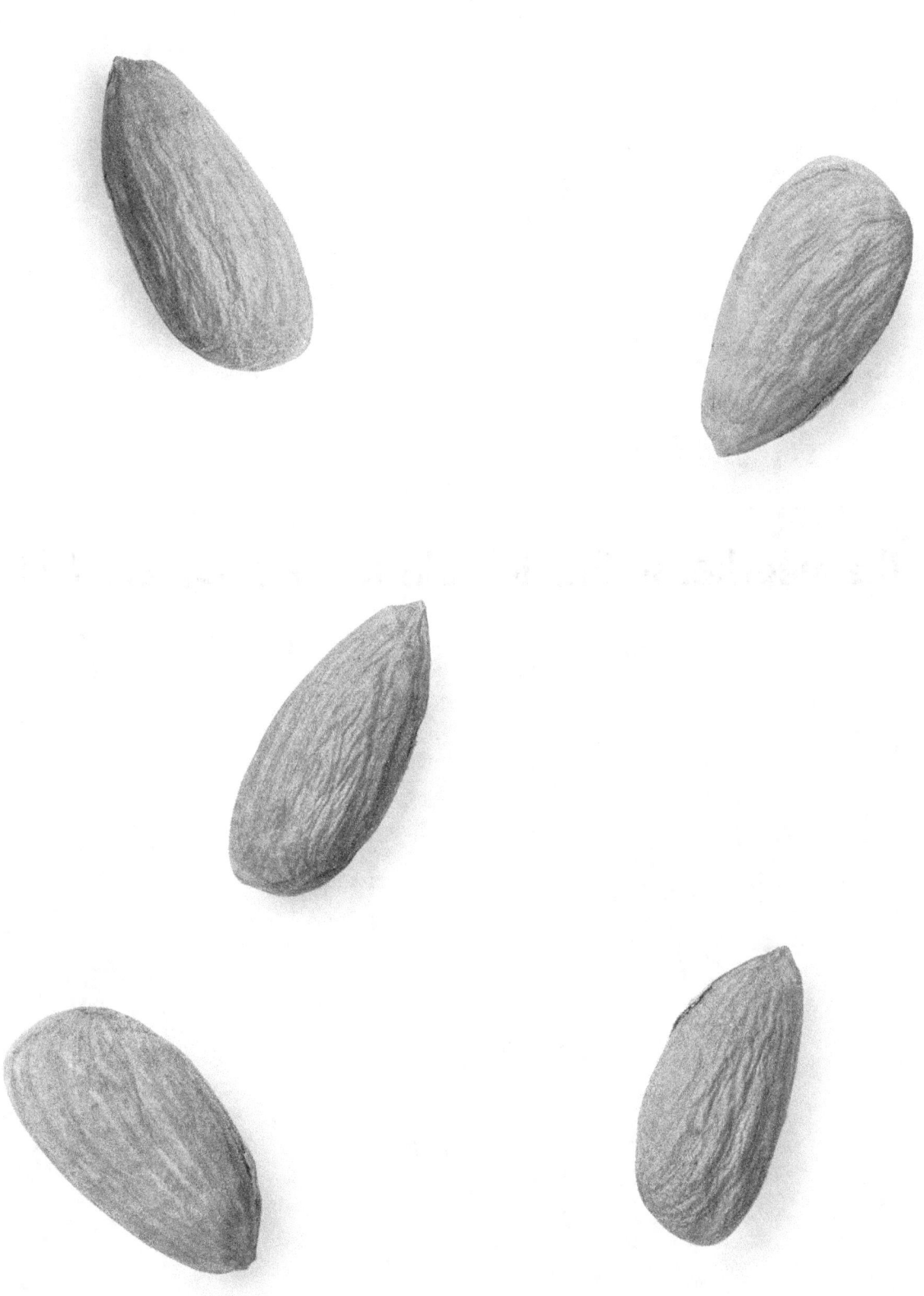

Dress the meerkat so that it looks like a Southern Belle.

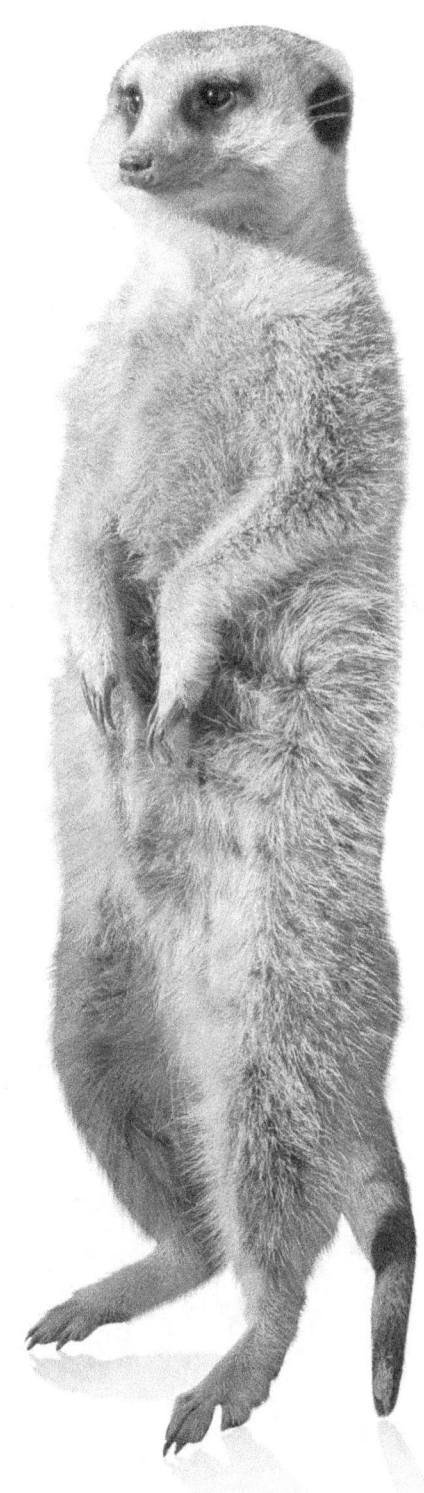

Add the lost city of Atlantis to this underwater scene.

Turn this beaver in to a lumberjack.

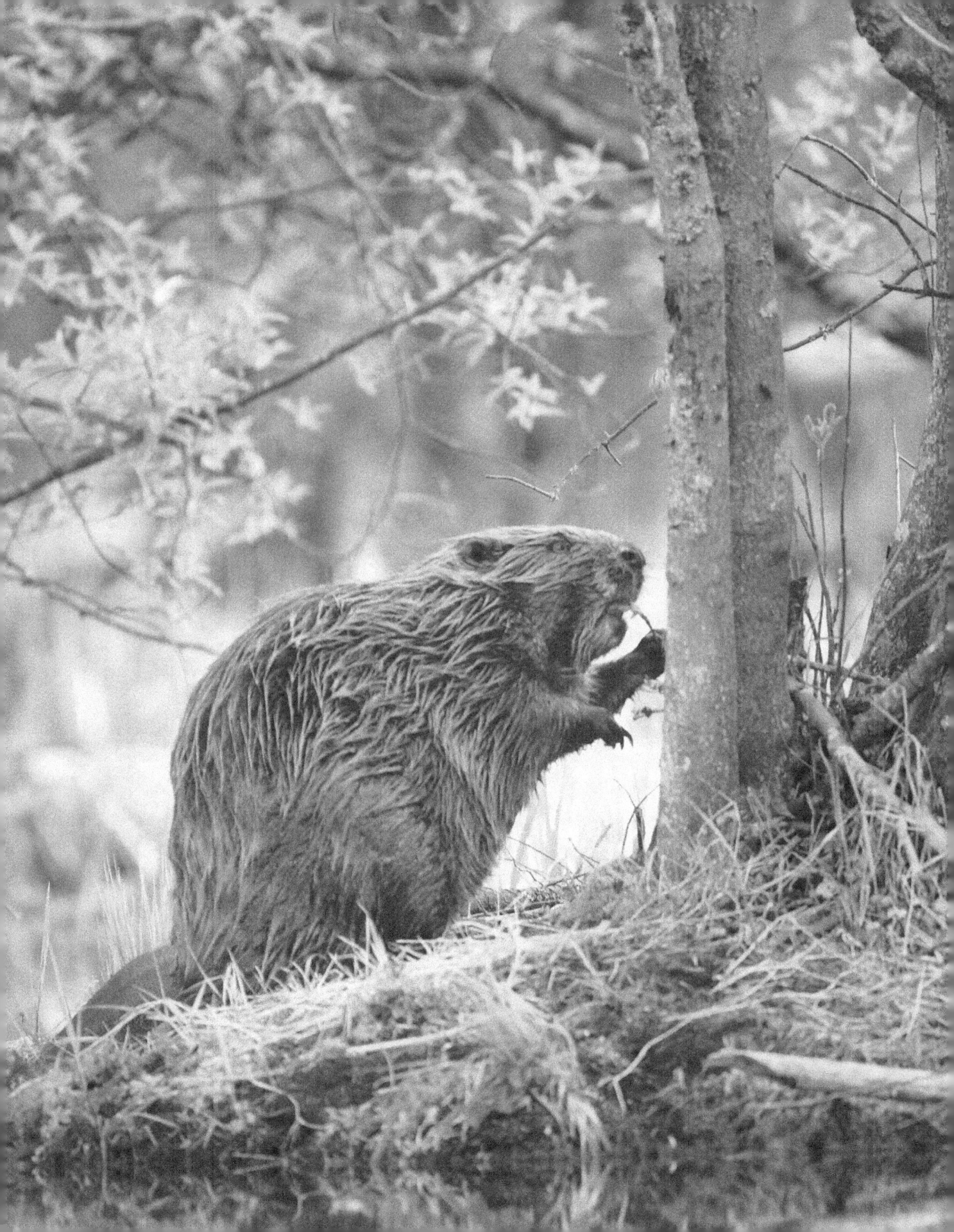

Turn this Dachshund in to a baker who is making some delicious dog biscuits.

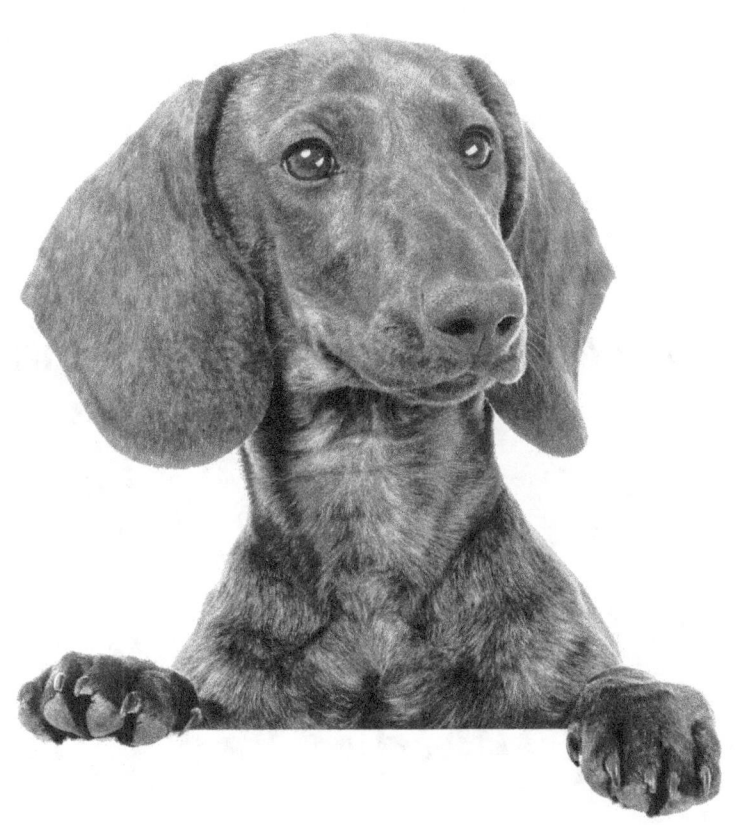

Draw a creature enjoying pretzels from the food cart.

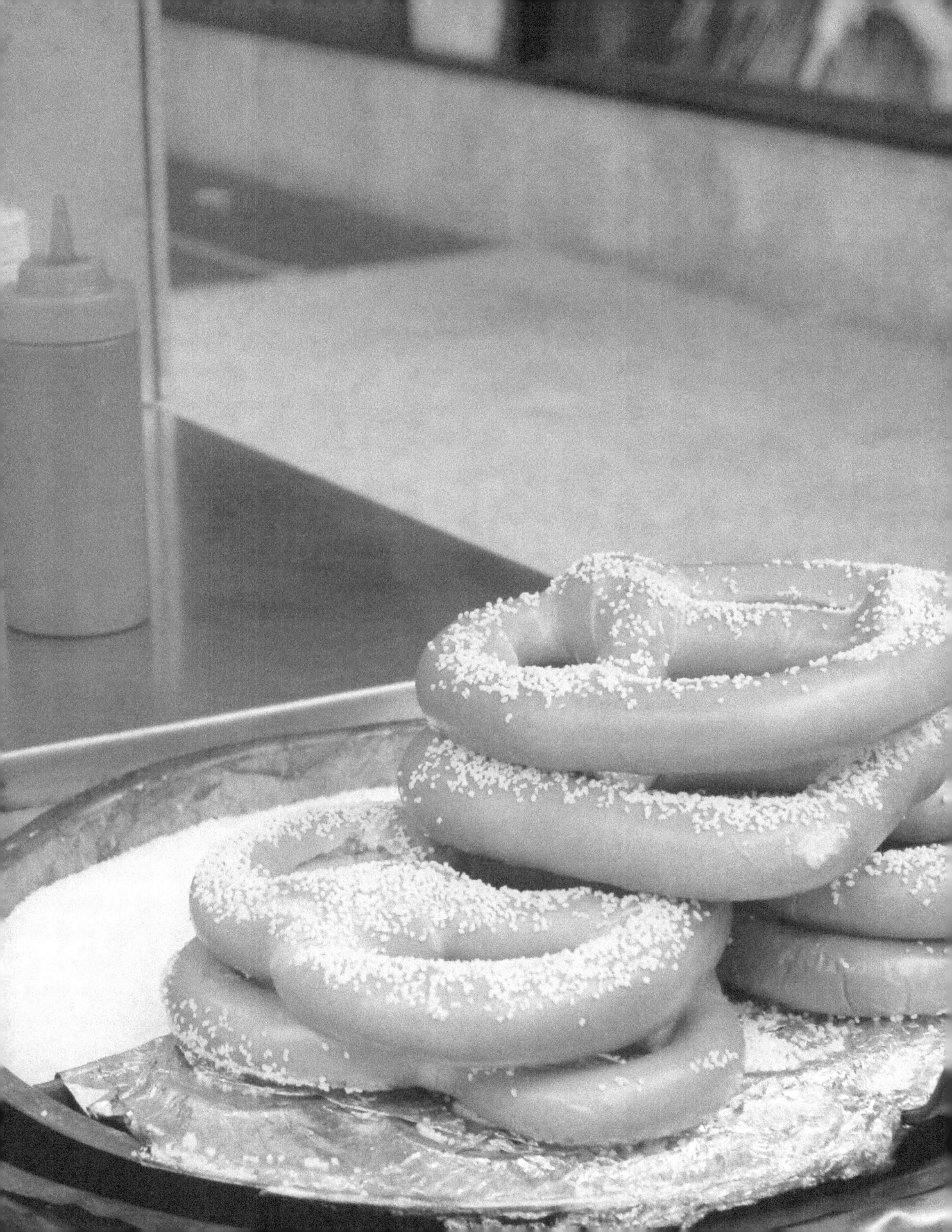

Draw a swimsuit on the monkey.

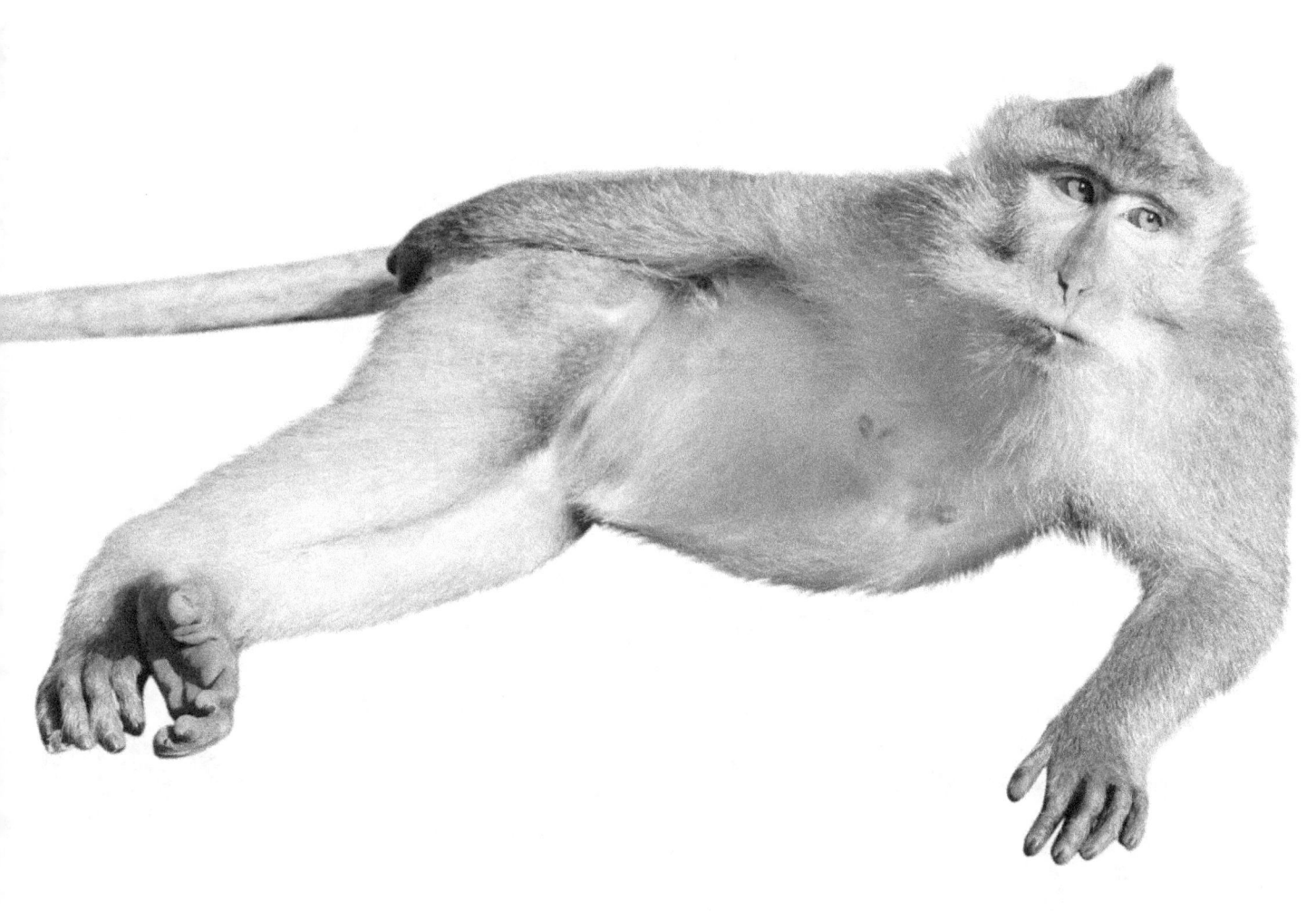

Turn this cat in to a skydiver.

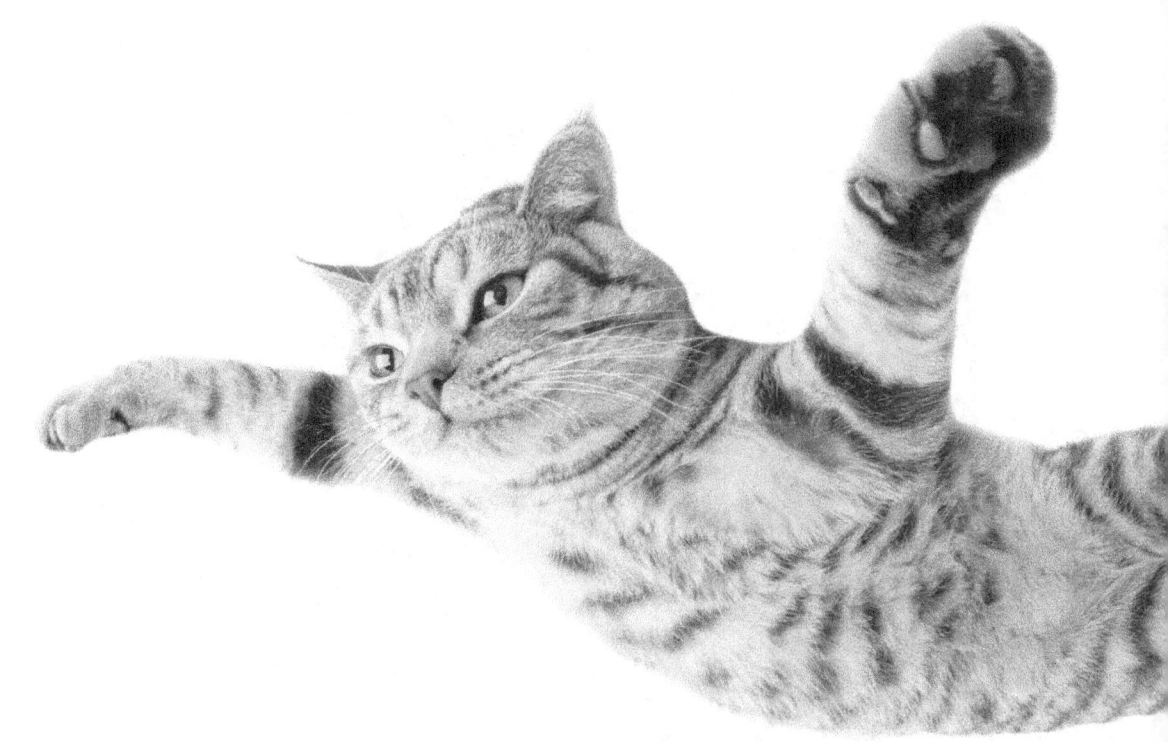

Add more buildings to this gingerbread town.

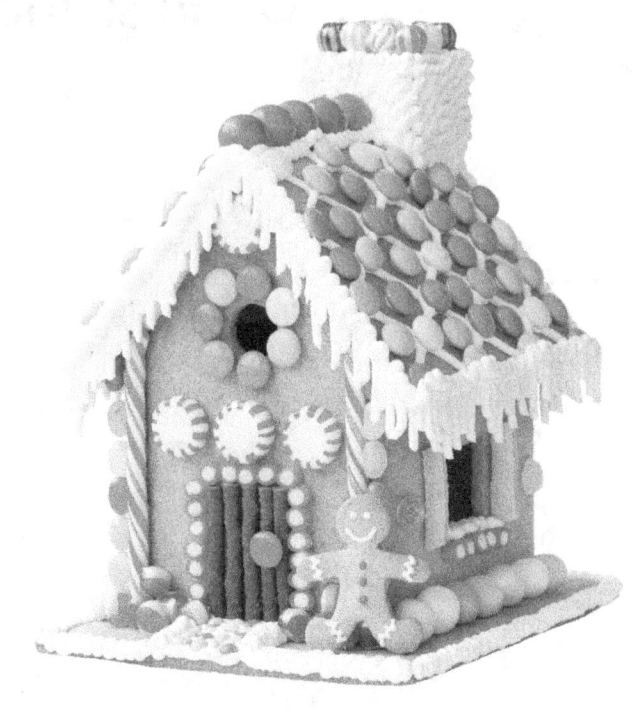

Give this sunflower a very silly face.

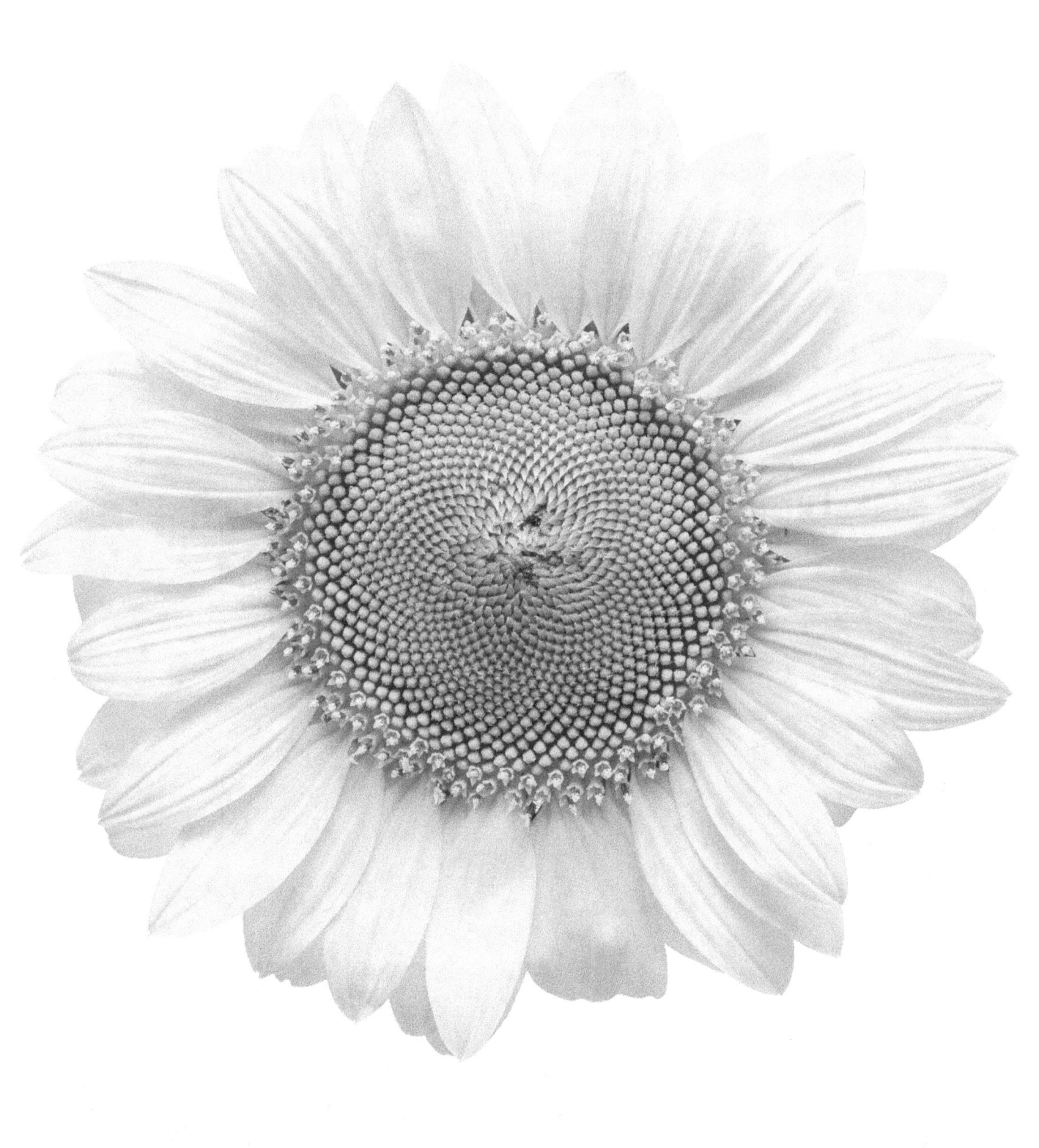

Turn this bear in to a fisherman with a
big bass on the hook.

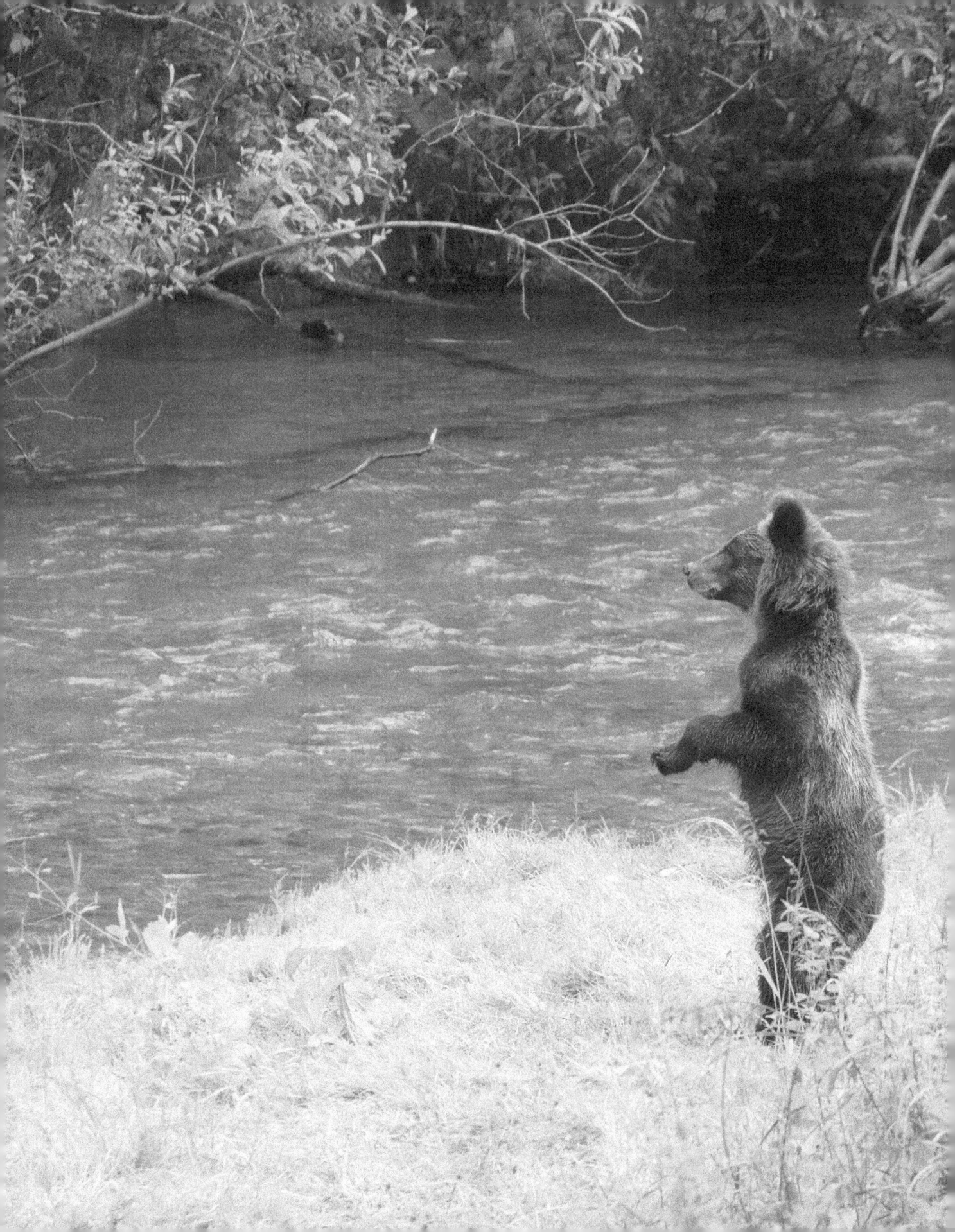

Turn this raccoon in to a deep-sea diver.

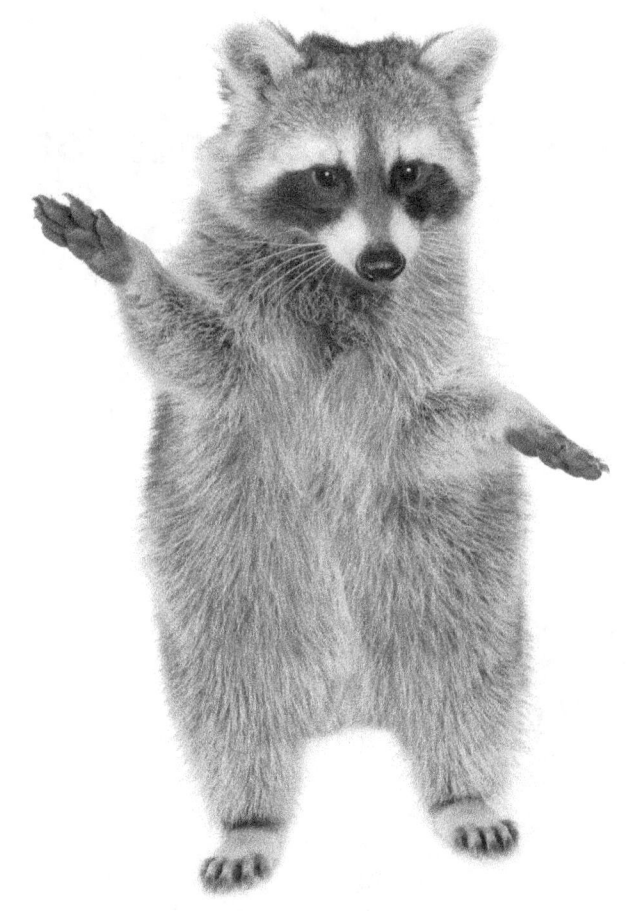

Draw a clown car that has stopped for some fuel.

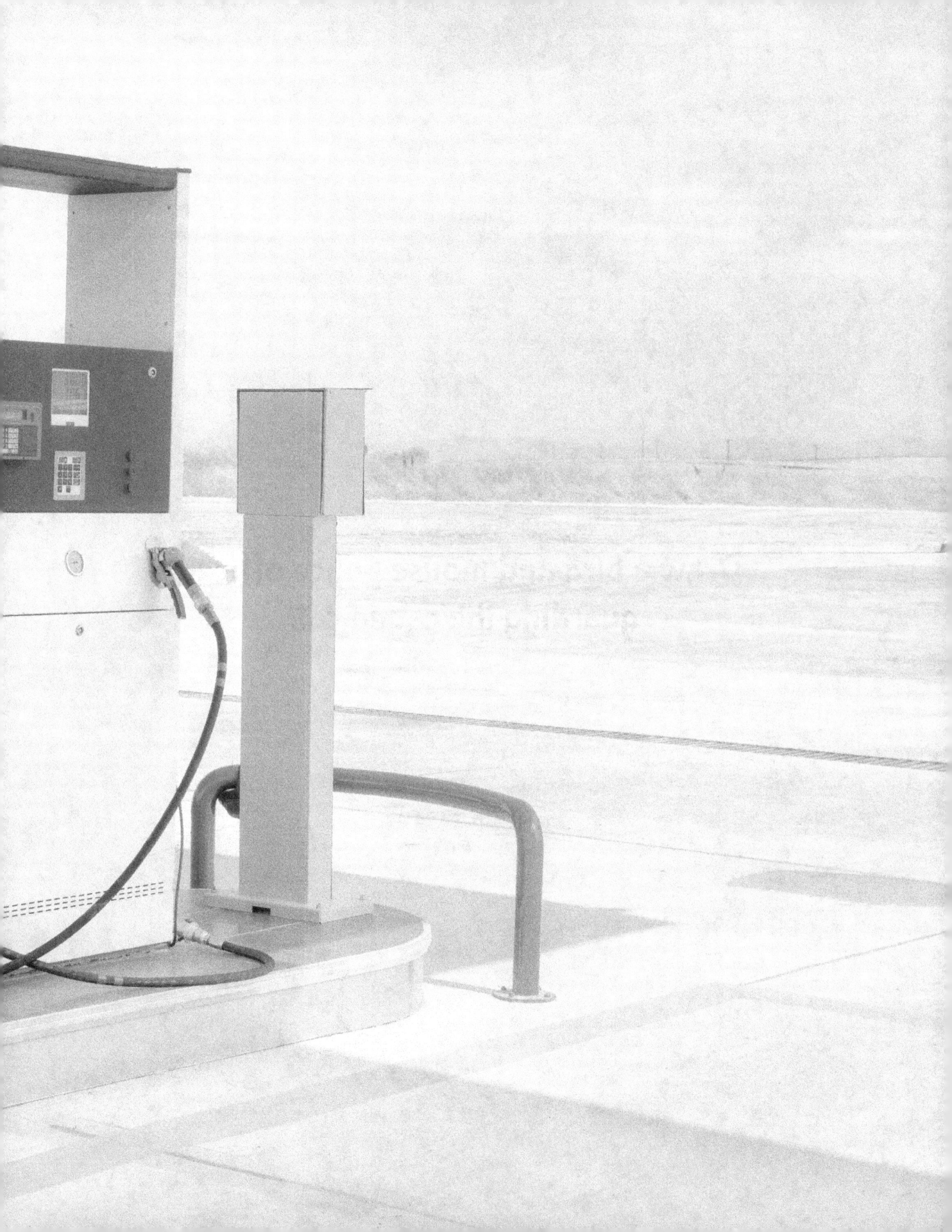

Draw a bird and mouse police officer guarding the caged cat.

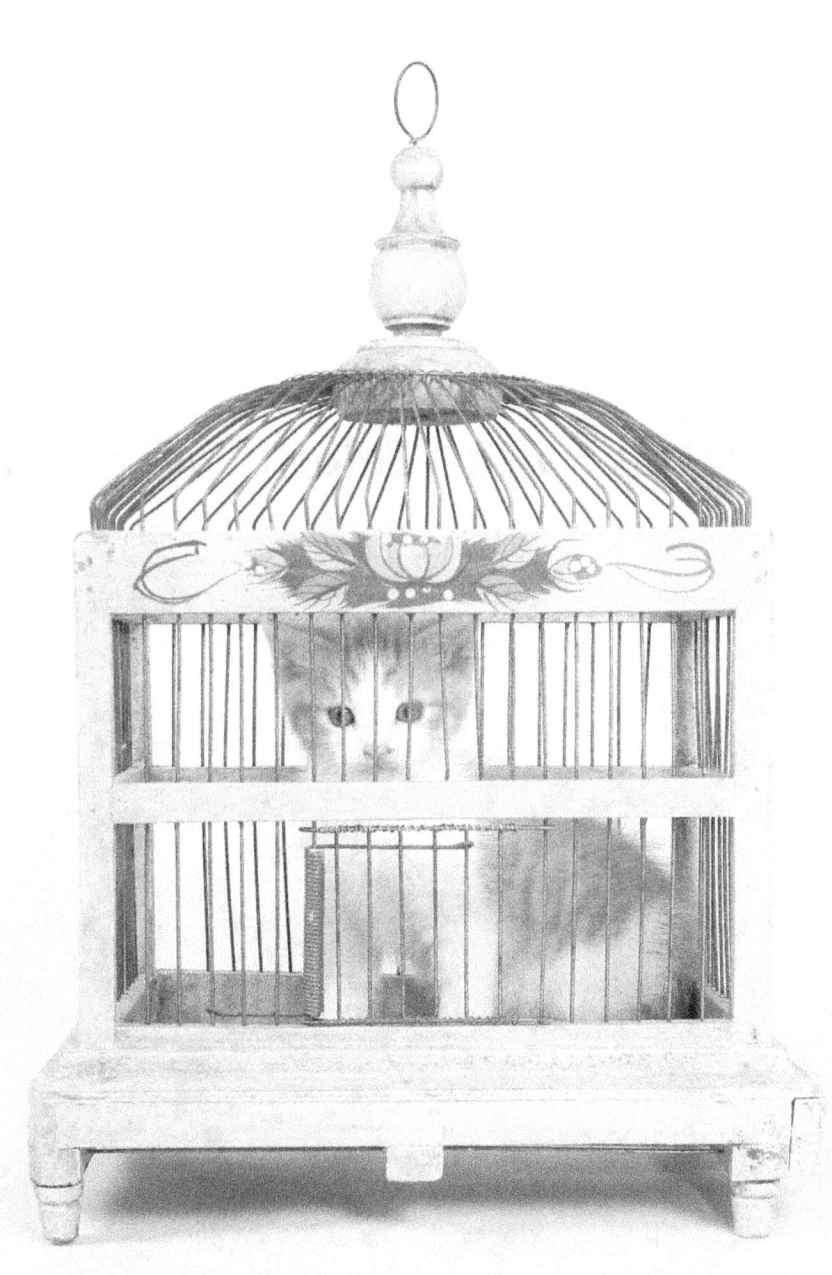

Give this horse a colorful beanie and a bowtie to match.

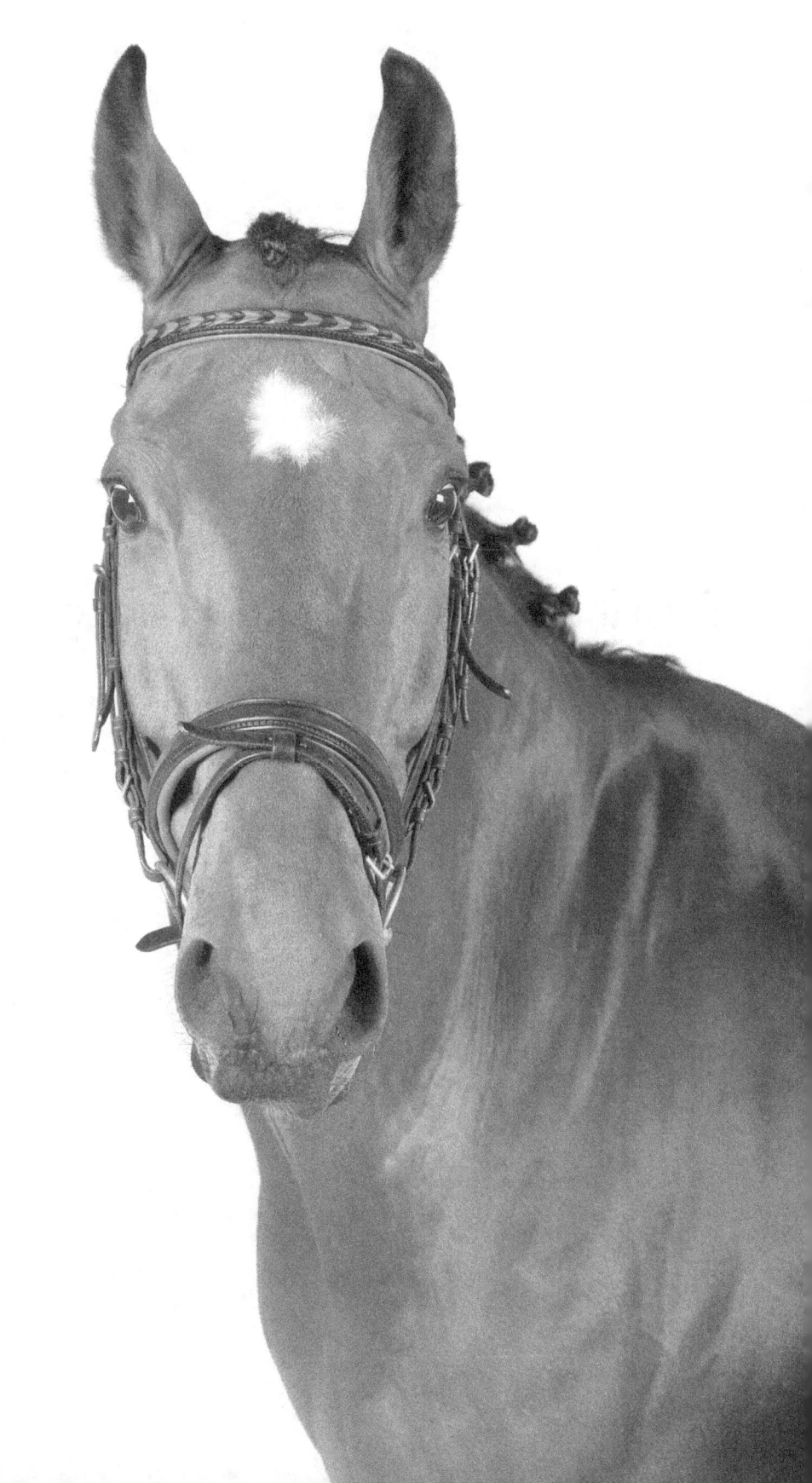

Turn this polar bear in to a skier gliding down the slopes.

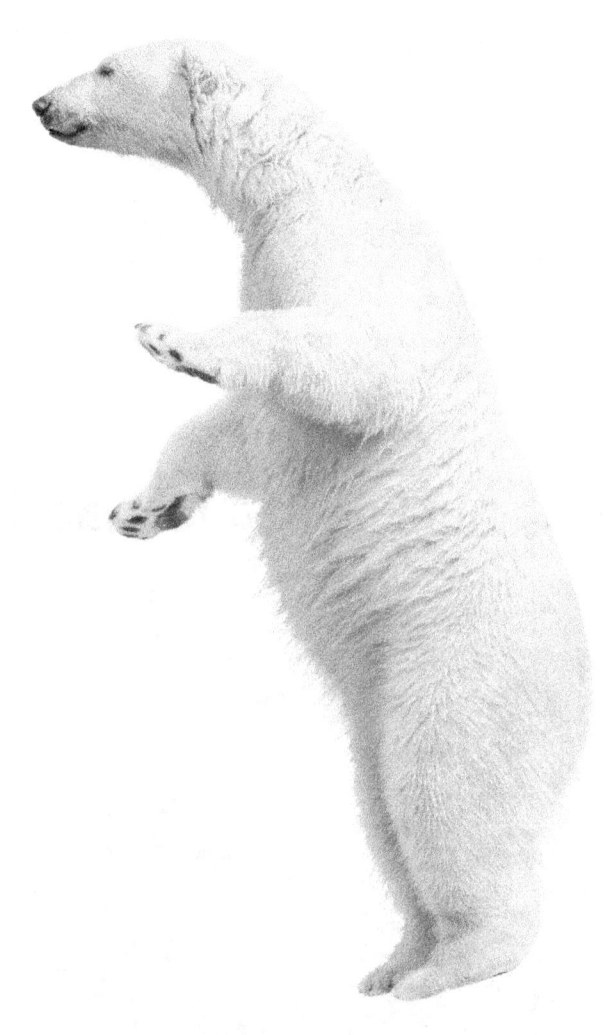

Turn the chipmunk in to a mariachi player.

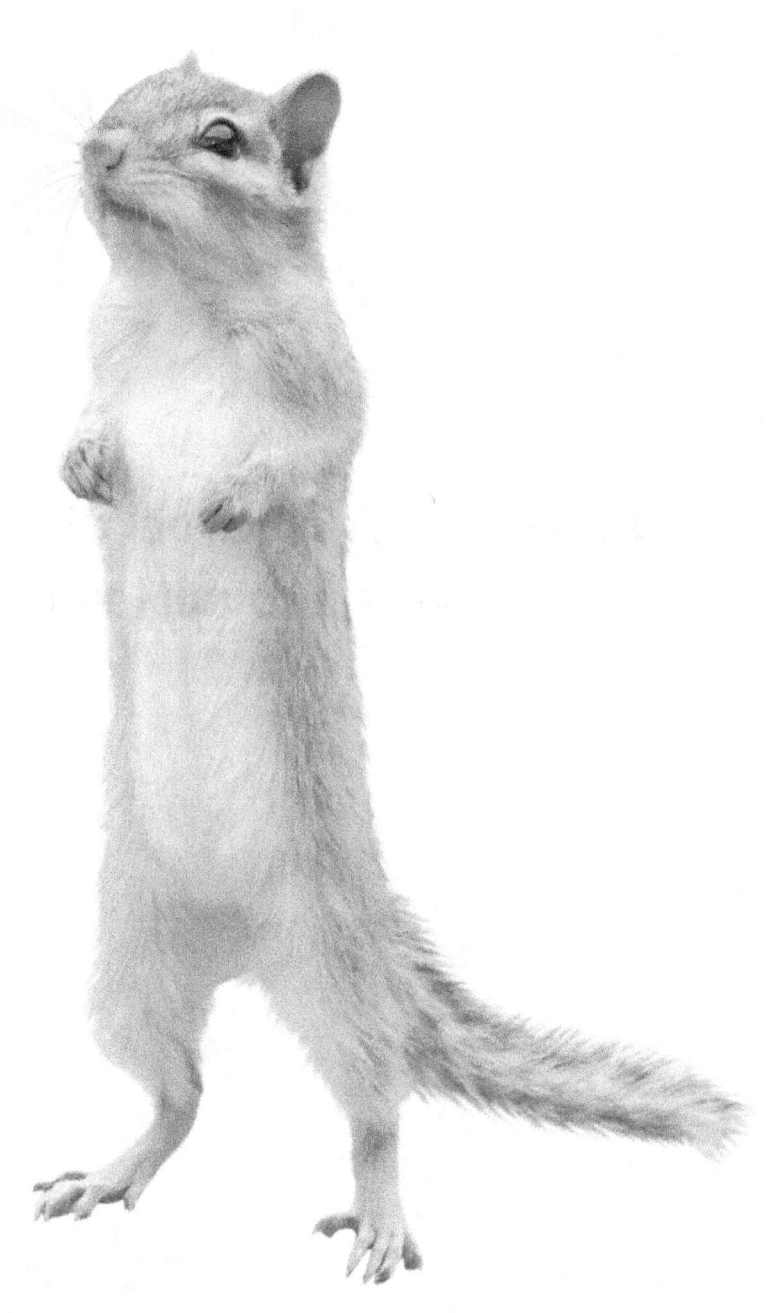

Draw a girl taking her pet dinosaur for a walk through town.

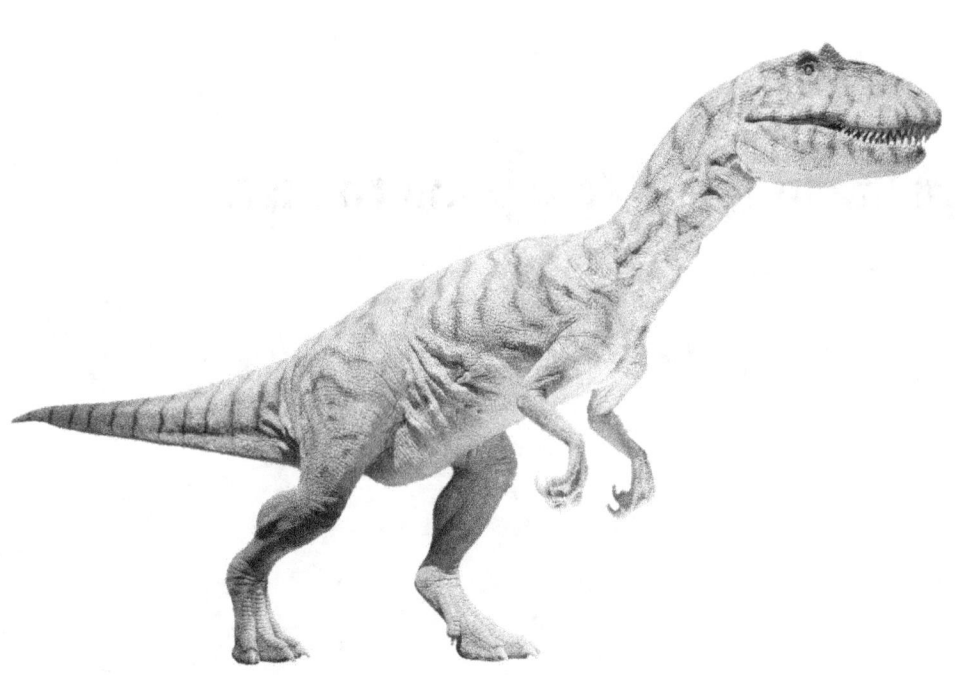

Transform the kitten in to a punk rocker.

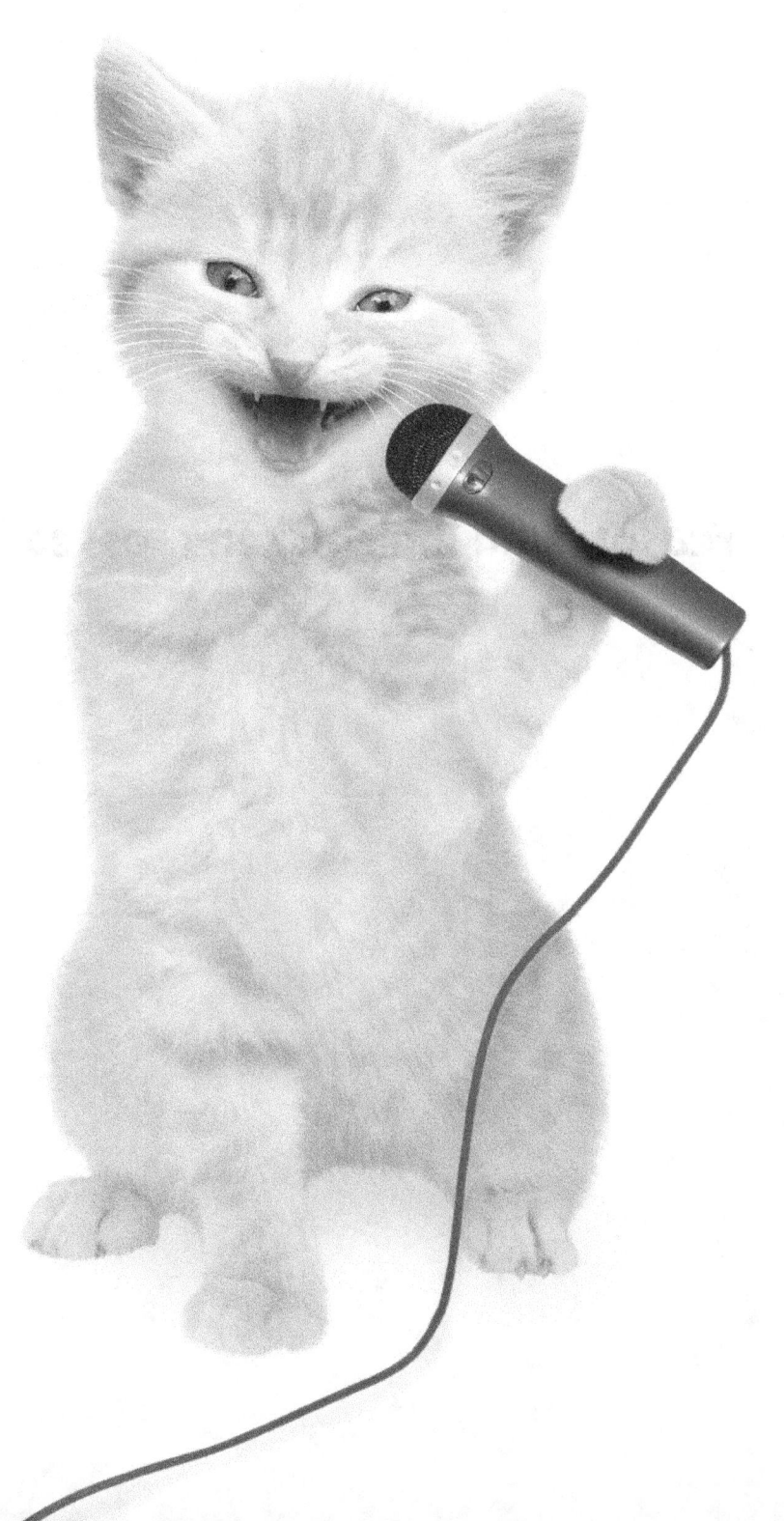

Draw the reason why the chicken crossed the road.

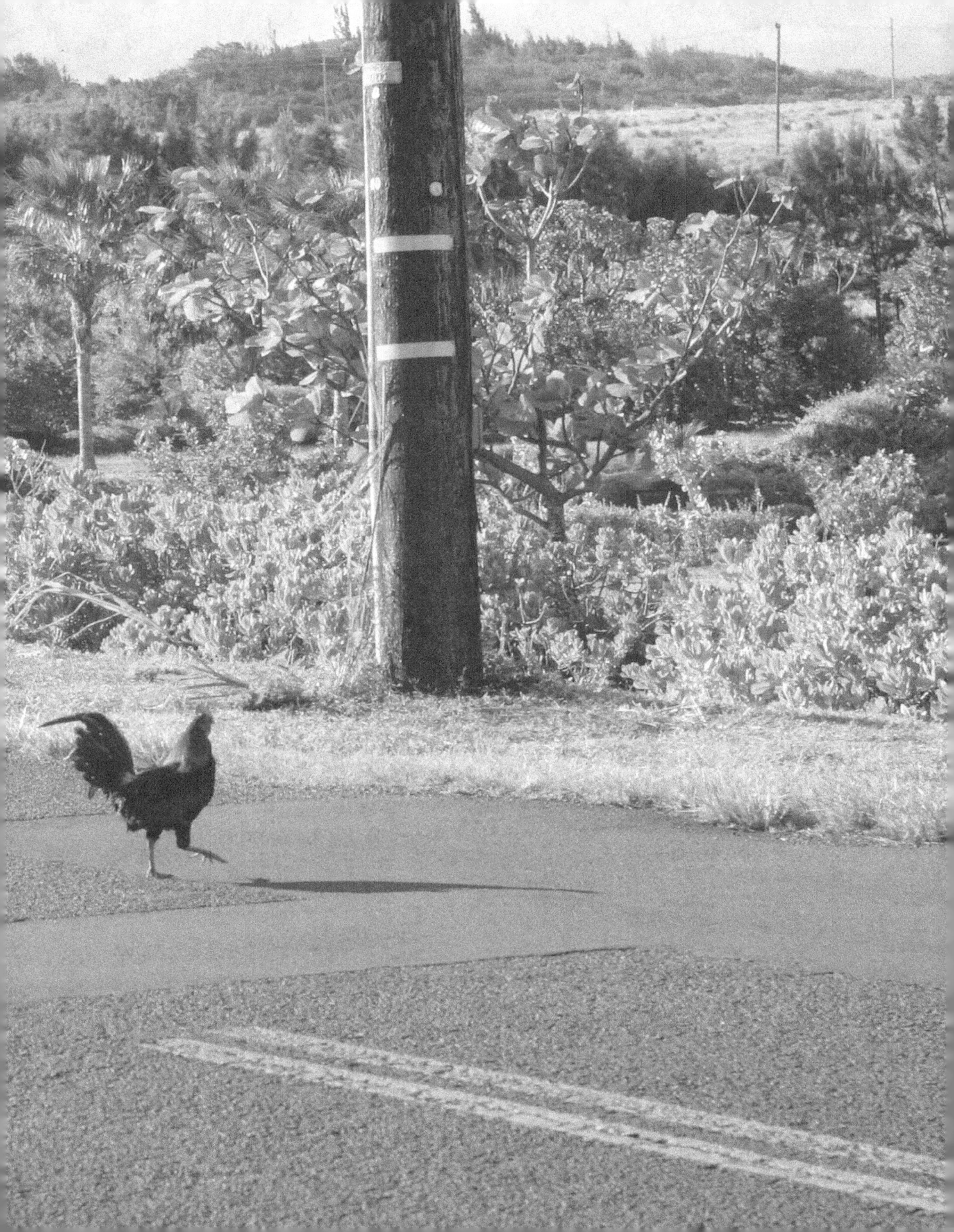

Draw some ice cubes and lemons jumping from a diving board in to the glass of lemonade.

Draw a water—skier being pulled along by a dolphin.

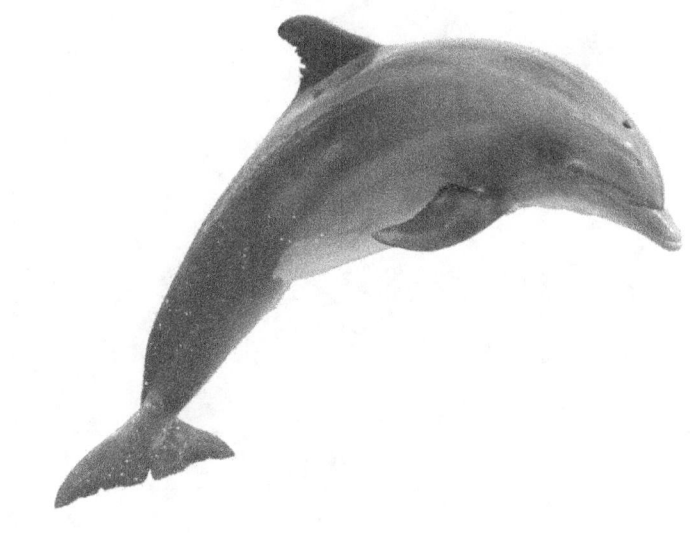

Dress the lion in a business suit.

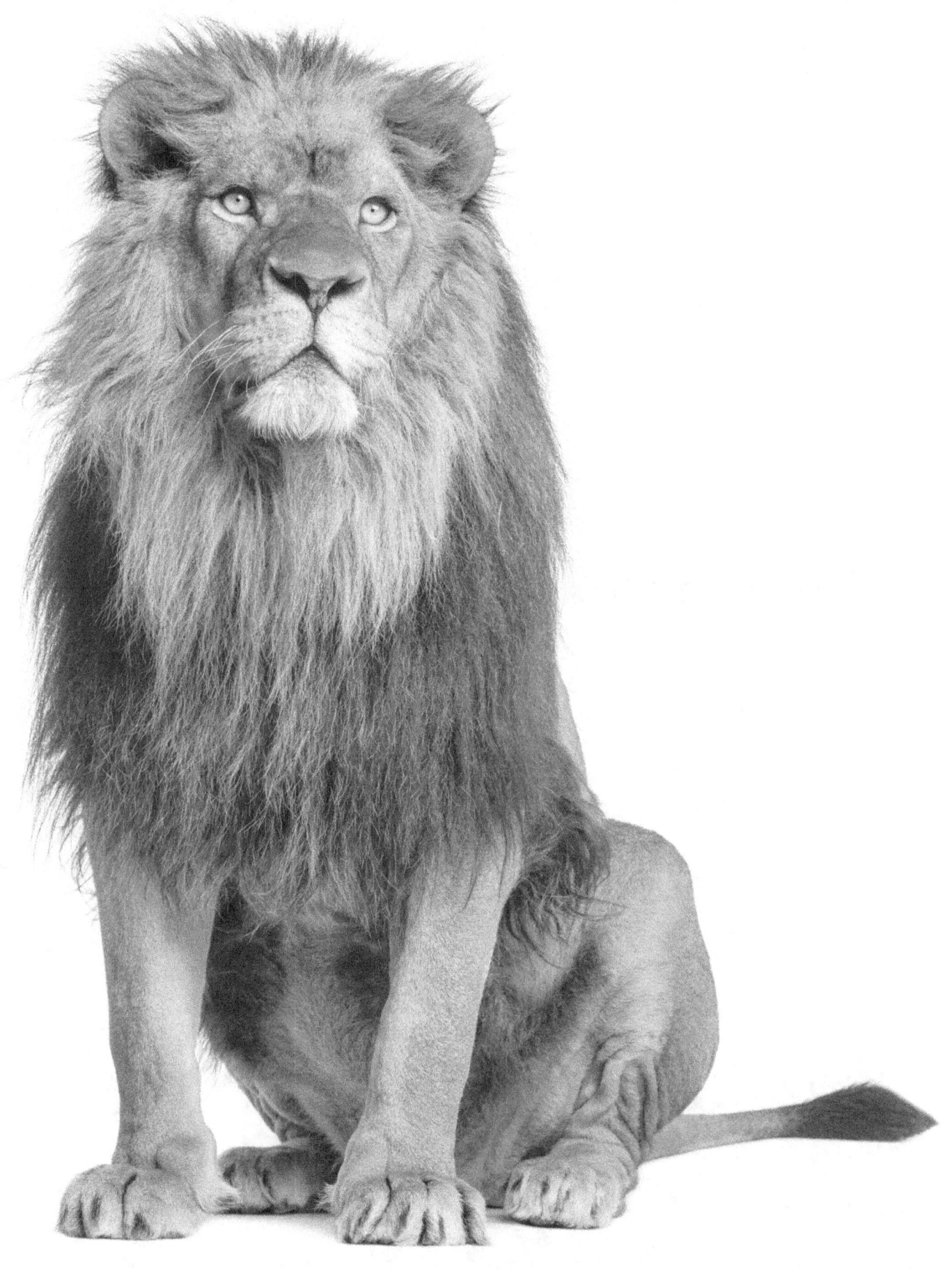

Turn the pig in to a surfer who is riding the waves.

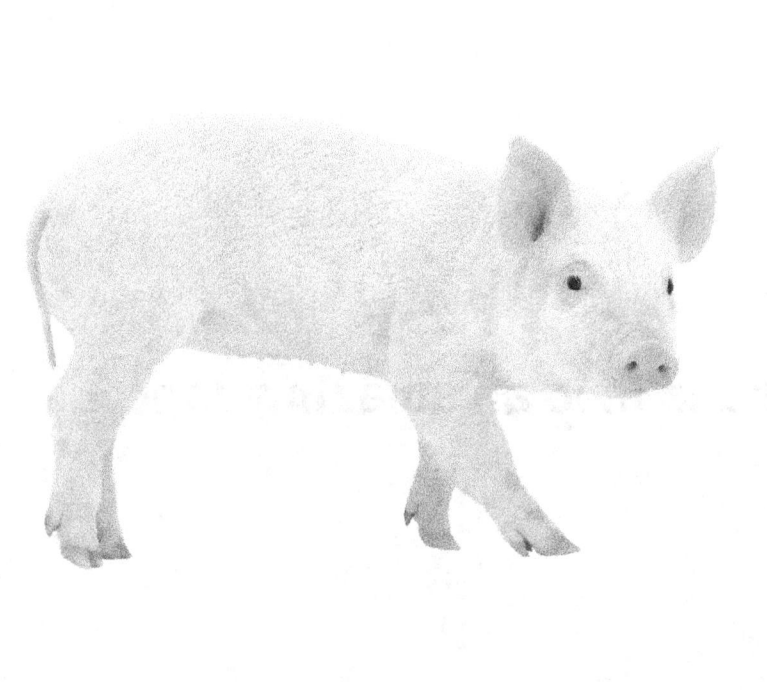

Turn the banana in to an amazing dancer.

Draw a rollercoaster for the otter to ride.

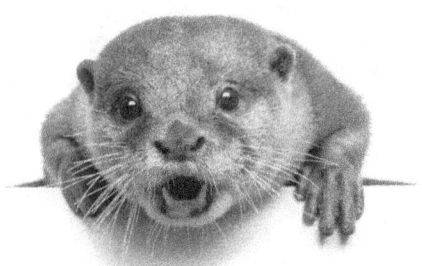

Dress the dog as a cheerleader.

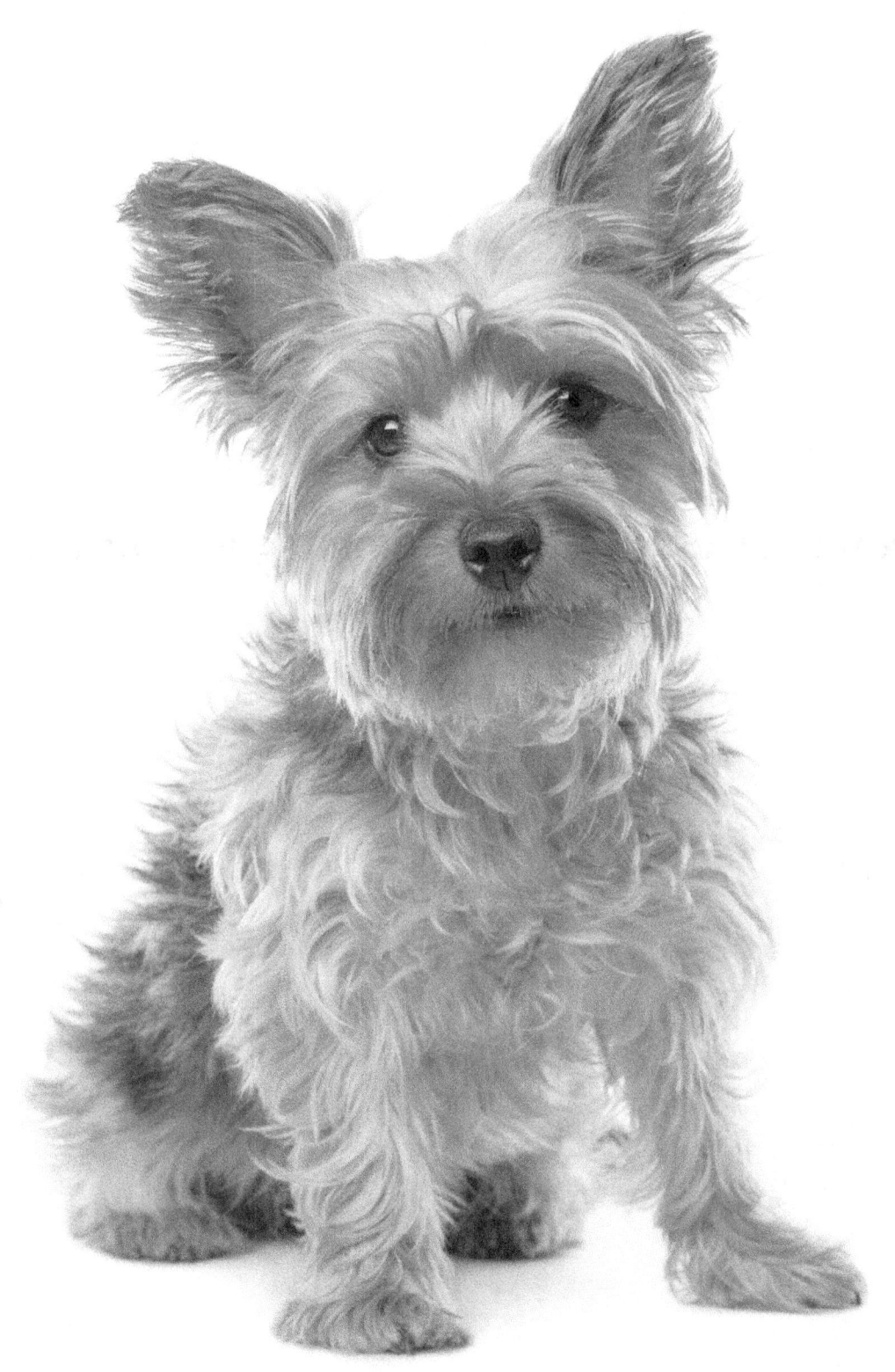

Draw the Loch Ness Monster swimming in a bowl of soup.

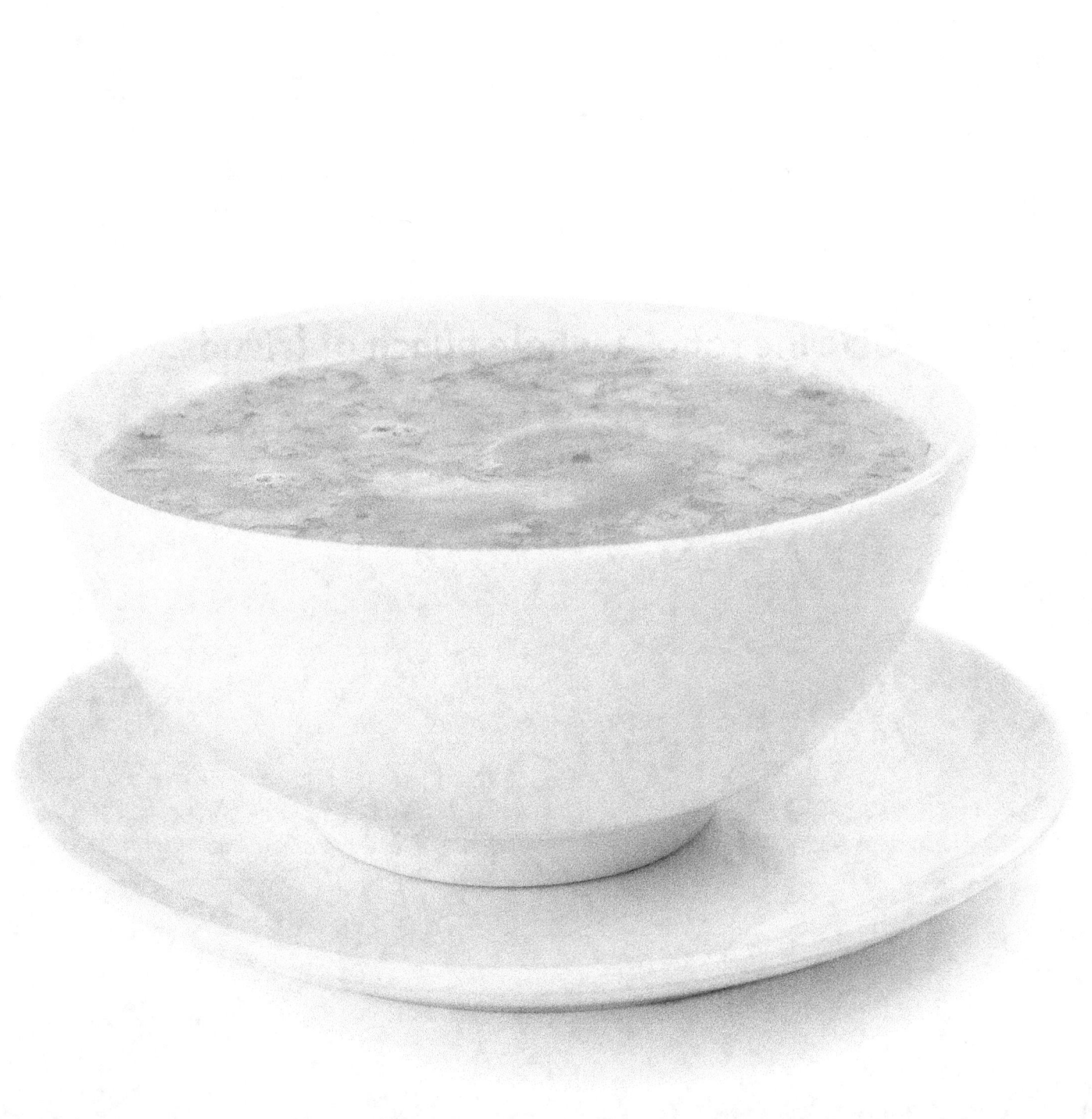

Give the robot a whole bunch of friends.

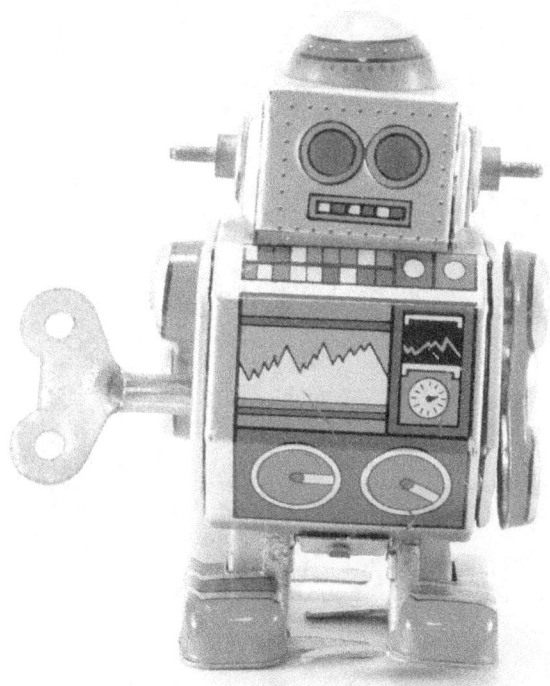

Draw the hedgehog rolling down a bowling alley.

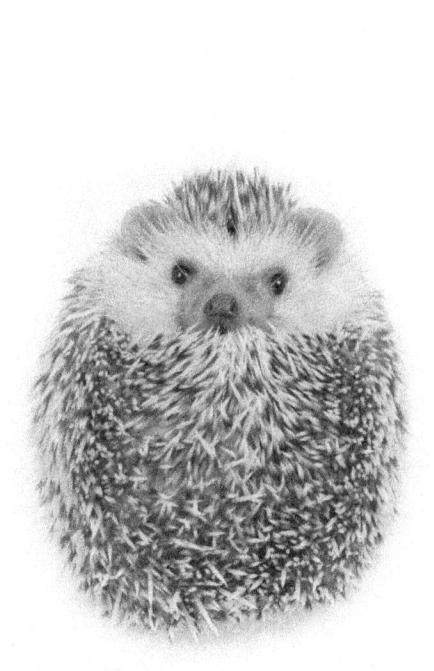

Draw a carousel horse for the lioness to ride.

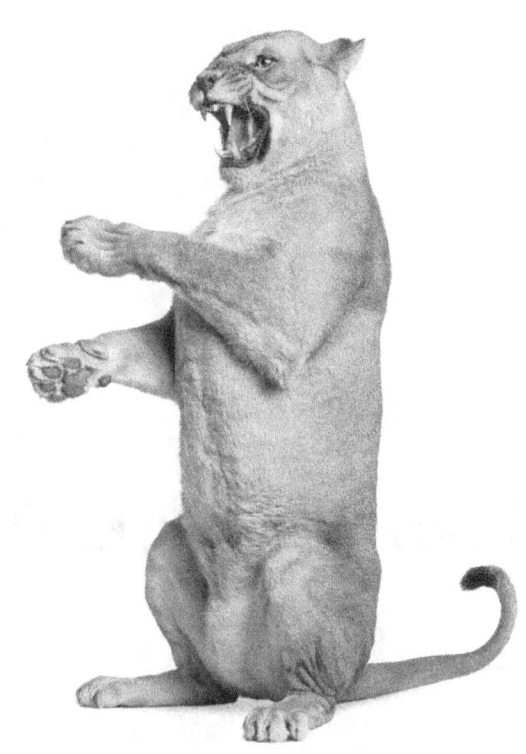

Dress the deer in an ugly holiday sweater.

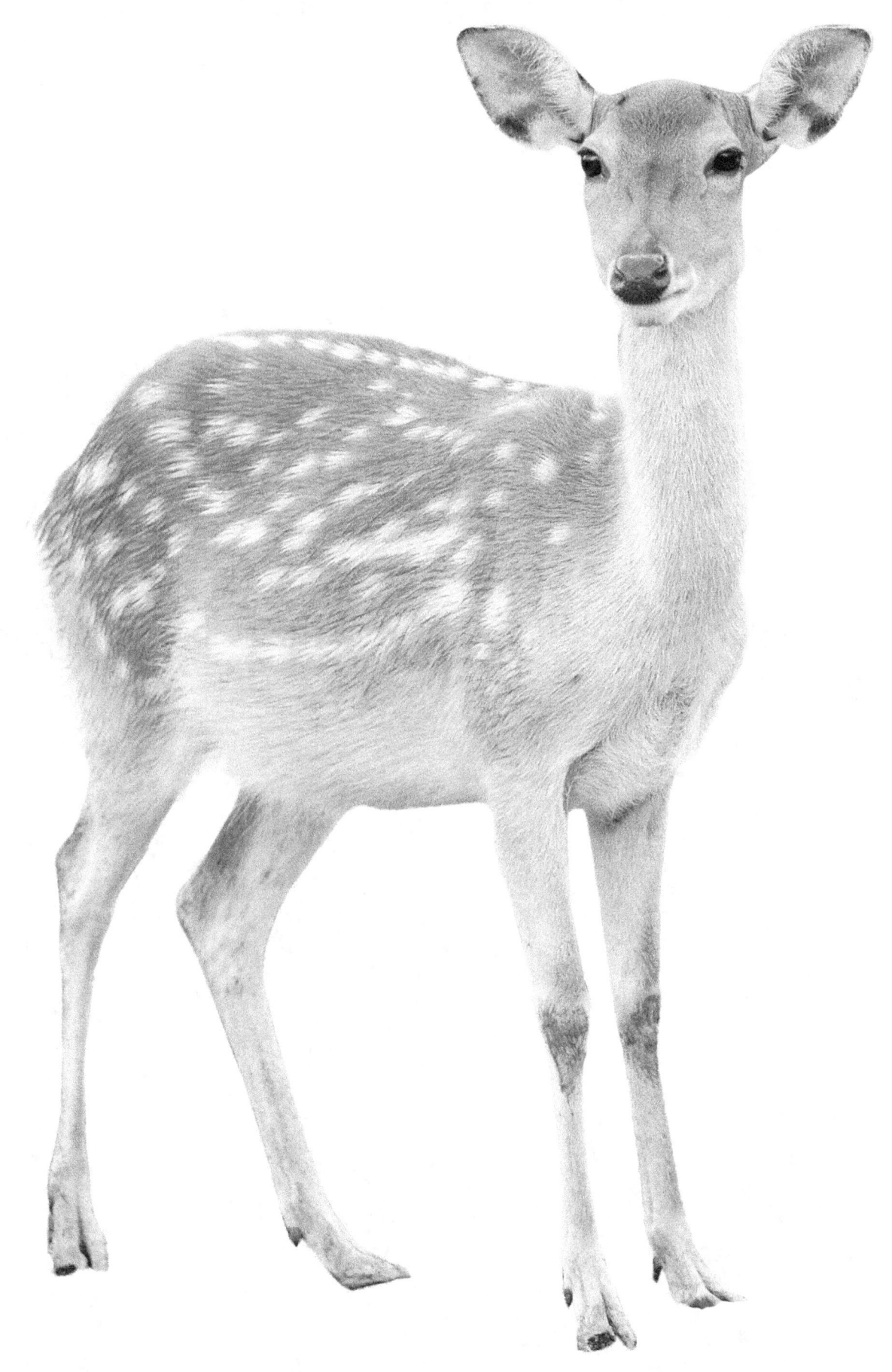

Put the cow in a muumuu and some fuzzy bunny slippers.

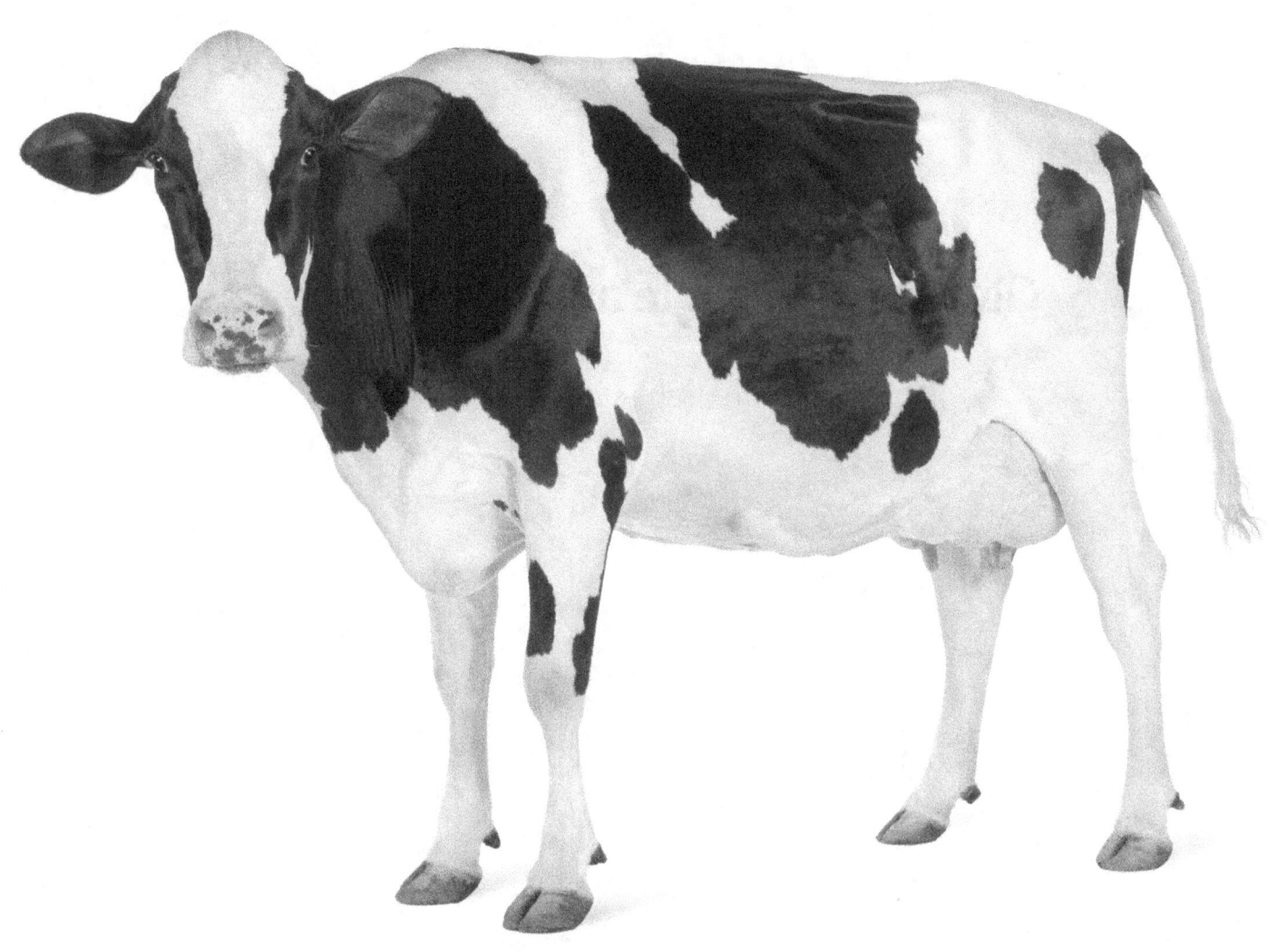

Give the bald eagle an obvious toupee.

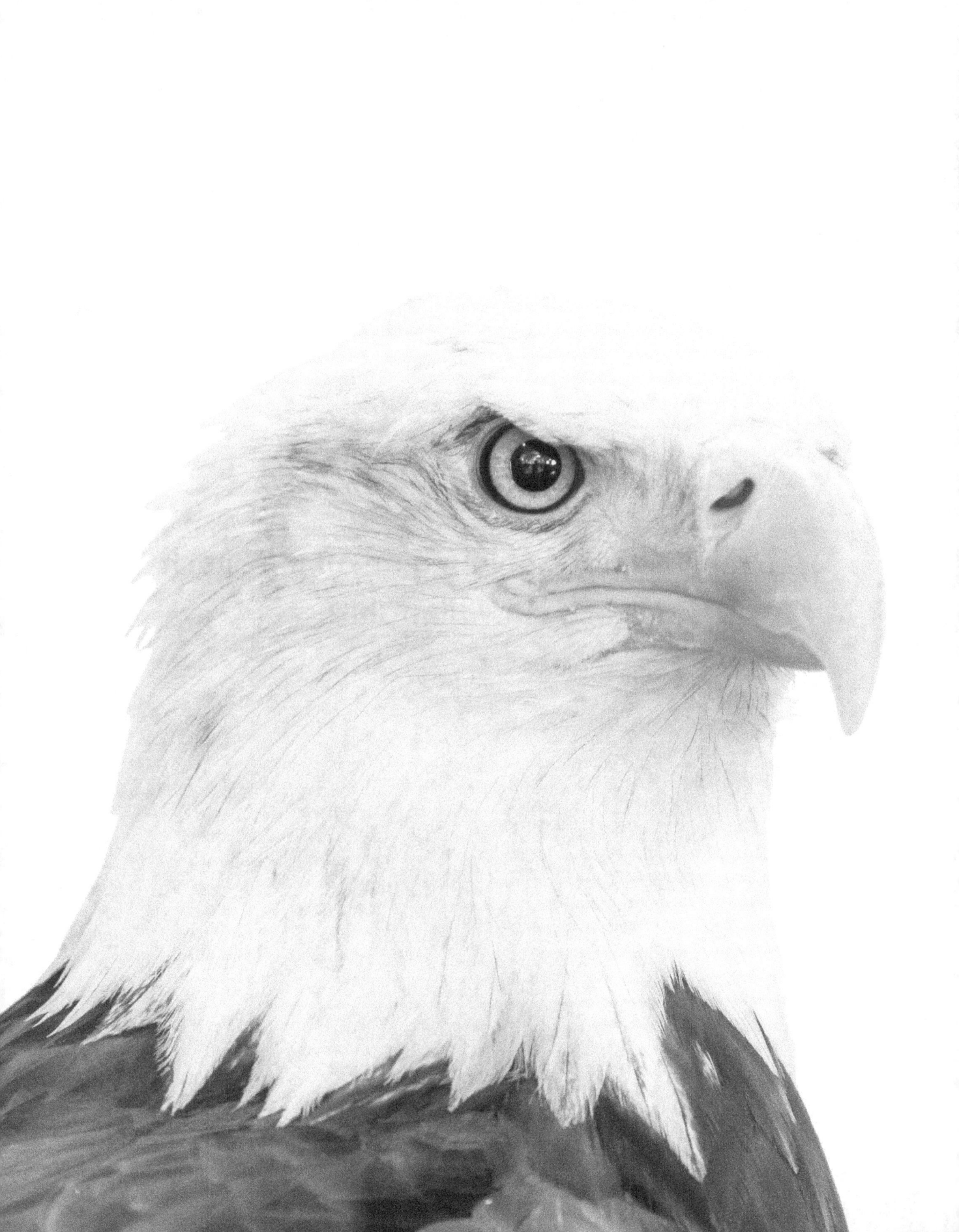

Draw the meerkat lounging on the beach in a Hawaiian shirt.

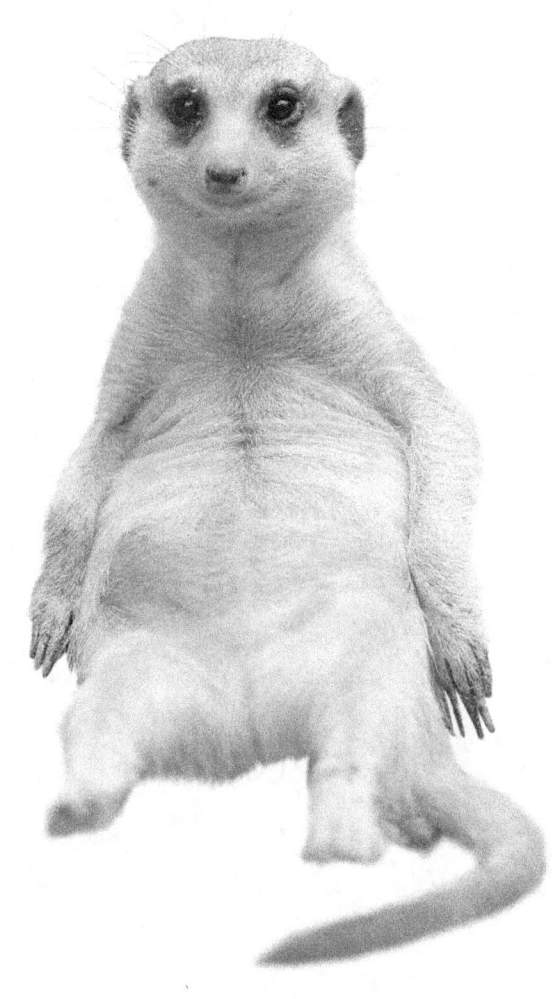

www.ingramcontent.com/pod-product-compliance
Lightning Source LLC
Chambersburg PA
CBHW080910170526
45158CB00008B/2059